Measuring Business Performance

Mick Broadbent

The Chartered Institute of Management Accountants

Acknowledgements

Several people have helped with the preparation of this book. I should like to thank the Chartered Institute of Management Accountants for allowing me access and the use of materials from their publications, particularly those written or edited by J Williams, R Scarlett and J Coates. I am also grateful to Marilyn Pritchard who has converted a series of draft manuscripts into a readable and presentable form.

Copyright © CIMA 1999
First published in 1999 by:
The Chartered Institute of Management Accountants
63 Portland Place
London
W1N 4AB

ISBN 0 7494 3500 9

Contents

Preface

The primary aim of this book is to bring together a series of themes regarding the developing issue of corporate performance management. It is aimed at all managers and professionals who are concerned with performance issues and who wish to consider an aggregate view of such measures and to map the current thinking in the area.

The book considers particular perspectives regarding corporate performance management. A major theme is the move towards non-financial performance criteria from the accounting-dominated financial measures of the past. Other themes reflecting the changing nature of modern organisations will include moves from the functional to the task based, from the individual company to the whole value chain, from the operational to the strategic and from the product to the customer.

The overall focus is towards the performance of the business as an entity rather than the detailed performance and control mechanisms that form part of its internal information systems.

The book brings together various themes and models that have been developed within companies, both by consultants working in the field and by academics. In many cases the actual origin of any particular theme or model may be difficult to recognise, as the company performance measurement agenda is one which crosses boundaries traditionally separate. The academic references made in the text are presented after the final chapter.

Introduction

Each of the nine chapters in this book takes a particular theme or series of themes for development. Each can be considered within the following simplified framework which links stakeholders, performance measurement and internal business processes together (see Figure A). The elements will be considered in turn.

Stakeholders are those constituencies that participate in sustaining the business through a series of exchanges; they include creditors and shareholders (financial exchanges), suppliers and customers (product or service exchanges), employees (labour and intellectual exchanges), and the environment (physical exchanges). Each stakeholder relationship must be managed by the focal organisation in such a manner to maintain, develop and enhance the exchange. Hence performance measures may be used to monitor, evaluate and compare such exchanges to ensure compliance, and achieve improvements and potential developments for the future.

Figure A: A framework for studying corporate performance measurement

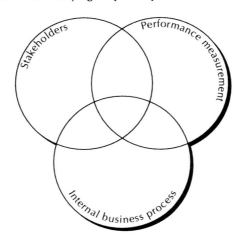

The performance measurement section of Figure A includes all internal and external measures that are employed by an organisation that reflect the requirements of the external stakeholders (customer satisfaction, return on investment, pollution avoidance, etc.) and those which are required to provide increasing efficiency and effectiveness within the internal business processes.

This section of the diagram is very much a 'catch-all' but the reducing boundaries between internal and external performance measures, the development of data-based information systems and the move to value chain based operations and strategies will mean a greater blurring of the internal and external performance measurement systems.

The internal business process part of Figure A includes the traditional aspects of strategic planning, management control and operational control (Anthony 1965), as well as all the aspects of modern management processes which are driven by the increased use of technology and the increased emphasis on the market and customer satisfaction in general. This will include the more recent techniques of total quality management (TQM), just-in-time (JIT), activity-based management (ABM) and business process re-engineering (BPR), to name just a few.

The diagram shown in Figure A provides a simplified structure for the studying of performance measurement, but in doing so, does not isolate issues from one another. Organisations are becoming increasingly transparent. Traditionally separate systems and procedures are becoming part of a whole, which leads to a natural overlap of the three elements in the framework, so ensuring that stakeholder issues are considered within internal business processes rather than being decoupled as in the past.

In terms of the structure of this book, the framework presented in Figure A will be used to introduce each chapter. This should help the reader through the various topic areas that constitute the performance measurement maze.

Chapter 1 views the changing nature of business and the changing nature of the management task. It considers the move towards technology-led, market-driven and customer-focused organisations, with the likely demise of functional management and the move to empowerment of all employees. In doing so, it highlights some of the changes that have occurred within the internal business process element of the framework and maps the drift of this element towards stakeholder requirements, thus hopefully providing a more reflective and adoptive series of business processes which will be considered in more detail later, and in Chapter 5 in particular.

Chapter 2 reflects on the traditional performance measures linked to financial reporting practices and the implications of such practices. Traditional reports reflecting financial performance measures have been largely decoupled from internal business processes save for the consideration of short-term 'bottom line' results. The concentration on the specific financial stakeholder groups has led to performance measurement being a product of legislative and regulatory frameworks rather than long term, decision relevant and broadly based.

Chapter 3 provides a link between strategic issues, critical success factors and key performance indices whereby key drivers of success can be recognised and managed. This chapter takes a normative approach to performance measurement whereby the internal processes of organisations' mission, objectives, strategy, critical success factors and performance measures can be placed in an almost cascading framework. This framework links business processes and stakeholder requirements through various critical success factor formulations.

The stakeholder perspective is taken in Chapter 4 where initially the focus of the shareholder is developed using techniques for measurement which include economic value added and residual income. These techniques are very much finance related and take the position that business processes' ultimate success can be viewed through the focus of financial performance measures. The techniques are currently in vogue. The importance of the customer as a stakeholder is also considered, as is the environment as an increasingly important aspect of management practice. These last two stakeholder perspectives provide a broader requirement for the development of corporate performance measurement and a balance to the financial orientation of the economic shareholder-driven models.

Chapter 5 brings two interlinking themes together. Both relate primarily to the internal business process element but have obvious linkages to the other two elements. The first is the critical resource perspective which views intangible resources within the firm as a critical success factor. The second is an overview of several techniques, including total quality management, business process re-engineering, just-in-time and activity-based management, which at first sight appear to be efficiency initiatives but provide mechanisms for organisational learning and hence the further development of intangible resources.

Integrated performance measurement tools are reviewed in Chapter 6, which includes the moves towards a balanced approach to performance measurement as well as the frameworks themselves. This chapter draws together several themes that have been developing within the text. The move is to integrated corporate measurement systems that consider various stakeholder groupings within the one framework, while considering both long-term and short-term perspectives and the internal business processes quite specifically.

Chapter 7 maps the linkages between business strategy and performance measures. The approach taken is to view the organisation as part of a value chain rather than in isolation. In doing so, it draws from the corporate strategy literature that considers the stakeholder perspective in a particular way that can be used as a vehicle to gain relative corporate advantage.

Chapter 8 develops the theme of external forces being important variables in shaping an organisation and its performance measurement systems and matrices through the contingency theory approach. This chapter provides a reflective narrative on the changes and developments that have been portrayed in previous chapters. It takes the theme that organisations require specific corporate performance measurement processes and systems to meet the requirements of their various stakeholders. The generic is not adequate, as each organisation is unique.

Finally, Chapter 9 considers the future role of the management accountant and the changing nature and ownership of the corporate performance measurement agenda.

1 The Changing Nature of Business

Introduction

Before considering the performance measurement of organisations it would be useful to review the manner in which companies and organisations in general are absorbing the various pressures for change. These pressures arrive from varied sources but each requires the business to provide an adequate response. The responses are generated by management who are required to provide enhanced performance whilst improving and maintaining quality, remaining competitive and sufficiently flexible to meet the next pressure for change.

In terms of the framework put forward in the Introduction and reproduced as Figure 1.1, this chapter mainly considers the internal business process aspect. In doing so, it reflects the increasing pressures from the broader and more demanding stakeholder groups whose demands are being integrated into these business processes. Organisations are creating corporate performance measures that encompass these demands to move the organisation forward. This latter step will be developed in subsequent chapters but is referred to in the last part of this chapter where results of a recent CIMA survey are presented.

Figure 1.1: A framework for studying corporate performance measurement

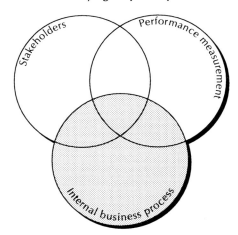

Drucker (1988) suggests that management is in its third development stage. In phase one, ownership and control were separated as shareholders appointed a separate cadre of experts to manage their interests. Next, managers introduced bureaucratic techniques and systems to administer the business, culminating in the multidivisional form of large companies. The third and contemporary phase is the shift to an information-based organisation, where managers facilitate and empower.

The transition to the third stage has been difficult for management accounting in general and performance measurement in particular. Many functionally based, financially biased reporting practices have been found to be lacking. New performance measurements that address customer satisfaction, competitive advantage, flexibility and productivity are required.

Changes affecting business

Whittaker (1992) considered the changing nature of the British economy, and highlighted three aspects in particular: the dramatic decline in the manufacturing base as measured in employment and proportion of gross national product; the boom in the financial services sector of the economy; and the growth of services concerned with outsourcing. Each is the manifestation of how businesses have reacted to different environmental stimuli.

Ezzamel et al. (1995) consider three major themes that have provided the momentum for organisational change. They can be classified as governmental, technological and managerial.

Governmental

The general reduction of both trade and capital barriers between developed countries has meant that each economy, and business therein, has been subjected to increased competitive pressures. National borders no longer provide a security of markets for domestic producers and service providers. Instead, multinational companies (MNCs) are creating cross-border markets which can move goods and services rapidly from market to market. Just as the market for real goods and services has globalised, so has that for money and capital flows. International financial markets are increasingly efficient, enabling finance to be transferred rapidly from country to country to reflect the movement of physical goods and invisible services. Hence, MNCs are free to move productive and service capacity relatively easily from country to country.

Technological

Developments in computer technology have led to improvements in information systems and changes to automative technologies which have aided the management innovation processes. The improvements to information systems include the manner in which data is collected, analysed and presented. There has been a shift away from financial measurement as the major source of information to more diverse sources, often in real time, which reflect the manufacturing technologies with which they are associated. The role of the monthly financial report is less important, as other information systems have already provided primary performance measurements. The monthly financial report merely confirms and formalises what has been reported previously in a more diverse manner.

The changes to automative technologies include the use of computers to control machines, computer-aided design, computer-aided manufacture and the ability to introduce flexible manufacturing systems. Each has provided a mechanism whereby processing and manufacturing speed can be increased with reduced labour inputs and improved quality. In parallel, these improved technologies also provide inputs into the information systems. Such change has meant that performance measurement systems are less concerned with inputs than they are with quality, manufacturing speed and flexibility.

Managerial

The last twenty years has witnessed significant change in the managerial process. Influences from Japanese management ideas and management 'gurus' have led to a reflective approach by managers who are seeking mechanisms that will accommodate the greater emphasis now placed on flexible manufacturing systems and quality provision.

The three themes recognised by Ezzamel et al. (1995) have resulted in a powerful momentum for organisational change. This has concentrated management thinking towards meeting the pressure for improved results, a greater customer orientation and the application of computer technology. Organisation change has gone hand in hand with the adoption of managerial techniques that have aided the constant drive towards increasing efficiency and quality improvements.

Organisational structure

There has been considerable change within organisations. The imperative to reduce the cost base and to remain competitive has resulted in a reduced workforce and the focus of the managerial task.

There is a move away from vertical and divisional structures to cross-functional teams and task forces which are required to exploit opportunities and solve current operational and market-focused problems. The move is away from 'command and control', so associated with bureaucracy and hierarchical controls, towards 'facilitate and empower' models of management. The delayering of organisations facilitated and aided by the increased use of information technology has meant that organisations are not only leaner but also more creative and adaptive.

Ezzamel et al. (1995) summarised this changing nature as presented in Table 1.1.

Table 1.1: Projected developments in 'new-wave management'

The past relied on:	Future emphasis will be to:
Rules, regulations and supervision, e.g. a span of control	Flexibly appreciate contingency and ambiguity
Hierarchical control and a clear chain of command	Effectively develop human resources
Discipline imposed by management	Facilitate employee self-discipline
A mechanistic and directive approach to problem-solving	Problem-solve through participation
Single-function specialists and individualism or independence	Create multifunction teams through mutual dependence
Job descriptions with defined tasks and responsibilities	Continuously review a fluid series of renegotiated assignments

(*Source:* Ezzamel et al., 1995, p.29)

To change the emphasis of management to what is described in Table 1.1 as 'new wave', managers must adapt the corporate culture of their organisation and be sufficiently flexible to create and encourage interdepartmental and cross-functional collaborative activity. Managers should become facilitators who ensure that their staff are properly equipped and trained in order to reflect the continuous change required to meet the challenges of the markets.

Managerial techniques

The delayering of organisations and the outsourcing of specific services have been made possible by various management innovations that have aided these processes. These include systems for material requirements planning (MRP), just-in-time (JIT), total quality management (TQM), business process re-engineering (BPR), activity-based management (ABM) and advanced manufacturing techniques (AMT), which have introduced automation and continuous improvement cycles with the use of flexible manufacturing systems (FMS). Each should ensure a greater level of efficiency which can be compared through benchmarking. Such techniques have contributed to organisational change that has necessitated the weakening of functional boundaries and the emergence of a more project-focused, multi-task framework for managerial activities, which in turn leads to a change in the measurement processes and indices of performance measurement. They will be considered in some detail in Chapter 5.

Britain in context

Atkinson (1998) reported that the root causes of the UK's 40 per cent productivity gap with the United States are restrictive planning laws and excessive market regulations that stifle competition and enterprise. The report by McKinsey puts the onus on ministers, as well as on workers and managers, to undertake painful reforms to promote national prosperity:

Many of the regulations that affect economic performance exist to achieve legitimate social objectives, but McKinsey argues that there is a need to identify the related costs so that better-informed decisions and trade-offs can be made between social and economic objectives. As well as calling for wholesale deregulation, the report outlines five other areas for action. First, the government should preserve the UK's flexible labour market and its well-developed capital market, and ensure continued macroeconomic stability. Second, the government should develop a more robust competition policy. Third, it should make sure that UK companies are exposed to global best practice by, for example, encouraging inward investment in low-productivity industries. Fourth, the country should invest in skills. Fifth, it should dismantle barriers to entrepreneurialism and technological innovation.

The McKinsey report backs the government's claim that poor productivity is primarily responsible for car-maker Rover's difficulties, not the strong pound. It says that Britain's old car-assembly plants, such as Rover's crisis-hit Longbridge, have failed fully to implement the new 'lean' manufacturing techniques that are designed to eliminate unnecessary manual labour, maximise the use of machines and keep stock levels to a minimum.

Figure 1.2 uses a Horngren et al. (1999) framework to draw together some of the major themes of the new management approach. The framework places customer satisfaction as the key priority and then relates this to the themes of key success factors (to be developed in Chapter 3), continuous improvement (to be developed in Chapter 5), the dual external/internal focus (to be developed in Chapters 7 and 8) and value chain analysis (to be considered in Chapter 7). Each theme cannot be taken in isolation but must be seen as an integrated whole, in order to generate customer satisfaction and enhance competitive advantage.

Figure 1.2: Key themes in the new management approach

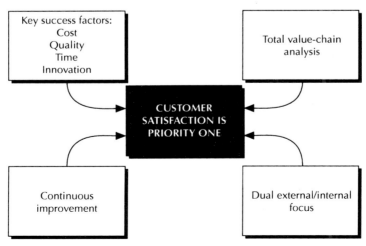

(*Source:* Horngren et al., 1999, p.14)

Changes to performance measures

Aggregate performance at corporate level as demonstrated in companies' annual reports has changed little over the last decade. The reports may reflect a greater need for compliance with accounting standards, corporate governance and legislative requirements, but in essence they provide a financial view of company performance. What is not reflected in the annual accounts are the changing managerial processes, technological innovations and requirements for continuous improvement. These are subsumed within the business activities which are required to generate those reported financial results. In many ways the reported financial results are a residual, that is, a measure of how well the business maintained its competitive advantage during the accounting period. Those financial results do not reflect the preparedness of that business to maintain its competitive ability in future accounting periods. Hence the need to ensure that internal processes recognise this longer-term aspect.

The changes to management processes and techniques which have been summarised in this chapter require a very different approach to performance measurement both internally and externally. The internal performance measures must sustain the requirement to remain flexible, the ability to build future competitive advantage and to be sufficiently integrative to provide a balanced view of the attributes of the business moving forward. A balanced approach to performance measurement is considered in Chapter 6.

Strategic issues

The manner by which any measurement of flexibility, competitive advantage and balanced performance is judged must be in relation to the strategy of the business. Hence business planning to meet strategic objectives and the measurement of the activities pursued to meet these strategies become two sides of the same coin. The narrow view of business performance so prevalent in financial reporting practices must be broadened to consider how the business enterprise and its management are reacting to the ever-increasing competition pressures in the market-place.

The manner of this performance measurement must be such that it reflects the particular strategic objectives of the different projects being pursued within the business. The term 'project' was used to reflect the changing nature of organisational life which is moving from the functional and divisional to a more integrative, cross-functional, task-based series of processes. As competition grows, so must the ability of the management process to create variety to meet that challenge. Hence the management of change becomes the central focus of any executive team. Strategic and operational change aided by the increasingly flexible use of technology, process management and information systems will be the imperative for successful business performance. A strategic view of performance measurement is put forward in Chapter 7.

What is and what ought to be

In a CIMA (1993) report on performance measurement in the manufacturing sector, it was reported that

> the questionnaire survey of SMEs and large companies suggests that wider use is made of financial rather than non-financial measures. In particular, the use of financial return indicators and working capital measures is widespread. Board members tend to be especially concerned with profit and return on capital measures and cash-flow projections, showing much less interest in non-accounting indicators. Providers of capital were interested primarily in financial measures and, to a lesser degree, general production measures. There was more emphasis within companies on non-financial indicators, focusing particularly on quality issues and marketing activities, and a general awareness of the different types of non-financial measures which they could potentially use, but these are nevertheless given relatively less weight than traditional accounting measures in the running of the businesses. This is in contrast to the literature, which of late has emphasised the monitoring of non-financial indicators.

Company executives show an awareness of and interest in the emerging variety of performance measure possibilities and, although the tendency is still to concentrate on traditional accounting measures, no aversion to adopting other approaches is indicated where this makes management more effective. As the standard literature suggests, companies will themselves take the lead in developing measures when they can see the benefits of so doing. There is no pre-established set of measures to guide the ultimate choice that companies make. The dynamic nature of the manufacturing environment will influence, on an ongoing basis, the types of performance measures chosen. Moreover, using this or that set of performance indicators appears not simply to be a matter of choice for many companies, because it is external competitive forces, such as supplier contracts or bid stipulations, that often place constraints on manufacturing output and these in turn get reflected in the different types of performance indicators which evolve.

This is an important finding of the study, because the suggestion is that the future of relevant performance measurement systems for companies is not in researching into comprehensive sets of appropriate performance indicators depending, say, on general manufacturing or competitive conditions. Rather, what is important is to ensure that manufacturers remain sensitive to the various options and possibilities, as they emerge, for using different performance measures to guide their enterprises' activities. Therefore, managers must remain current with general approaches to determining performance measures best suited to their needs and should develop their own judicious permutation of indicators.

In terms of the use of performance indicators by investors and lenders, it is clear that there is continued reliance on financial performance measures. This is not necessarily to be avoided. But what is of the essence is that bankers and other relevant external parties do not concentrate on financial measures in deference to tradition. That is, if manufacturers see the potential for better representation of their commercial affairs in terms other than purely financial, then lenders may also benefit from developing the same method of assessment of commercial viability, business rationale and financial risk. The engine that runs today's manufacturing environment differs considerably from that of ten or fifteen years ago. If manufacturing operational managers can see ways of managing more effectively by implementing changes in performance indicators, then lenders should get themselves on to the same wavelength. Those that do will thrive and be ahead of the rest. The case studies considered suggest that foreign bankers are often forerunners in this respect.

It has been noted above that manufacturers are keen to gain exposure to novel ideas about performance measures. Managers have a good understanding of traditional accounting indicators and, indeed, the following were widely used: sales, profit, margins, assets employed, return on net assets, capital expenditure, debtors and creditors, sales days in work in process. Dimensions of non-financial performance such as customer satisfaction, employee efficiency and quality levels were thought important by all companies surveyed, but not all had developed satisfactory methods of dealing with them. (p. 34)

Summary

This chapter has provided an overview of the many and varied pressures that are providing challenges for business organisations. It has also considered the nature and manner by which businesses are reacting to these challenges. The strategic viewpoint which can facilitate and drive operational change must be seen as an imperative if competitive advantage and hence superior or adequate performance is generated.

In contrast, the chapter has also stated the position put forward by the McKinsey report (1998) in which a variety of reasons are cited for weak corporate performance relative to other major manufacturing economies. As a postscript, the chapter concluded with a reflection of performance measurement in practice some years ago and the manner in which that can be progressed to meet future challenges.

The next chapter considers the traditional nature of financial performance measures and how interfirm performance comparisons may be made. This is seen as a necessary step prior to the introduction of more recent performance measurement ideologies in an attempt to amend the traditional.

2 Performance Measurement: A Reflection

Introduction

The first part of this chapter considers the nature of traditional financial reporting performance measurement. The basic techniques with their inherent problems are considered, as are the implications of adopting such narrow performance measurement approaches. The chapter then develops a series of formal comparisons that a company may make with its competitors regarding the determinants of performance. In doing so, it attempts to improve the processes which drive its own performance. The final section of the chapter firstly introduces a move towards a more strategically driven performance measurement agenda, and secondly one which considers the cash-flow aspects of the business's value which are both developed in subsequent chapters.

Figure 2.1: A framework for studying corporate performance measurement

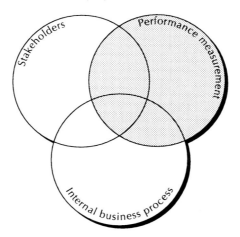

The main theme of this chapter is the consideration of the performance measurement element of Figure 2.1. The measures put forward are very traditional in nature and are bound up with the manner in which published financial reports have evolved. However, many of the financial measures have not changed significantly since the early 1920s. Figure 2.1 clearly shows an overlap between the three elements of the framework, but the theme of this chapter is very much on a series of performance measures that are narrowly focused, somewhat decoupled from the internal business processes and take a short-term view of the shareholder as the primary stakeholder. In later chapters this decoupling of the three elements will be revisited to reflect the current nature of the corporate performance measurement agenda and move away from the narrow financial (profit) focus.

The last part of the chapter considers other data sets for corporate performance comparisons, but these are not automatically linked to improvement mechanisms within internal business processes. They are more reflective than action-based, although benchmarking and product cost comparisons may be part of a more business process improvement agenda.

Profit measures

Any business can be viewed as an economic unit which employs resources to generate a return to its owners. A standard measurement of the outcome for the use of these resources is profit, which reflects the excess of revenue over expenses. The manner in which that profit is distributed to the owners of the business may be the subject of debate, but the financial outcome as represented by profit is a powerful measure of business performance. Absolute profit may be a measure of performance but must be linked to some measure of input to provide an index of efficiency that is comparable. Hence profit must be standardised in some manner. The two more popular managerial measures are to evaluate profit relative to revenue or capital employed, while the two popular financial market measures of profit are earnings per share and the resultant price/earnings ratio. The managerial measures should be established before the impact of the financing mix on the business, so providing a measure of asset efficiency rather than financing efficiency.

Profitability margin refers to the profit as a percentage of sales revenue. This has the advantage of relating the output of profit with the input of sales revenue, hence providing a measure of efficiency. It does not consider the capital employed required to determine that level of sales revenue. Return on capital employed does provide such a measure. It is the most popular measure of corporate performance as it captures all the attributes of inputs and outputs and hence is comprehensive in nature.

The establishment of a return on capital employed (ROCE) figure, which is also known as return on investment (ROI), is relatively simple for a particular business. It links operating profit with capital employed. Both are easily derived from the published annual accounts of any registered company. The manner by which ROCE and ROI can be used as a comparative measure for intercompany performance is not as simple.

Problems of applying ROCE and ROI

Both the dimensions for the above calculations are accounting derived. Both figures are the result of applying Generally Accepted Accounting Principles (GAAP) to the transactions of the business. As the GAAP process is designed to provide a legalistic and regulatory view of profit and capital employed, it means that any devised measure of efficiency, like ROCE and ROI, is subject to the conventions of accounting which may not aid economic measurement. In turn, each company interprets the general accounting conventions into particular accounting policies which are considered most appropriate for that particular company.

The performance measures of ROCE and ROI for individual companies become more difficult to compare with other companies, even in the same industrial classification. Specific problems include:

▪ the different valuation systems applied to fixed and current assets;
▪ the manner by which leased and other 'off balance sheet' assets are treated;
▪ the recognition of profit with regard to the capitalisation of research and development, interest charges for new asset acquisitions, etc.

Each of the above means that ROCE and ROI have to be standardised to eliminate different reporting practices in order for each company to be truly comparable with others. The standardisation process will be difficult, as each company may be unwilling to declare corporate-sensitive information to assist an agency to provide such standardised performance data.

The implications of ROCE and ROI being such popular measures of business performance may lead managers to pursue policies within the internal business processes which may be damaging to the business in the longer term. These include:

▪ The rejection of projects which are in the company's best long-term interests by having projected positive net present values but which may reduce the reported ROCE in the short term. The introduction and adoption of different performance measures may mitigate this problem: for instance, the use of the net present value of cash flows or residual income reflected in economic value analysis.
▪ Managers may seek short-term goals which lead to the overstating of the current year's profit and the understating of capital employed. Both will result in 'superior' ROCE figures.
▪ The representation of performance through the narrow focus of financial returns may lead managers to neglect the determinants which generated those financial returns.

Earnings per share and price/earnings ratio

Earnings per share (EPS) and the price/earnings (P/E) ratio are commonly quoted attributes of company performance by the financial press and used as symbols of company performance by those operating in the financial markets. EPS is established by dividing annual profit by the number of shares in issue during the year, while P/E is the current share price divided by the EPS.

The EPS is generally derived from the published annual accounts but adjusted by market analysts to be more reflective of ongoing company performance. The resulting P/E ratio, also known as the earnings multiple, represents the ratio of current earnings to the net present value of future earnings as represented by the share price. It is a mixed time period ratio, giving a link between the current and future anticipated earnings.

The EPS figure is not particularly useful in comparing company performances, but once standardised using the current share price of the company, as reflected in the P/E, it does contain a measure of comparability. However, the P/E is dependent on future earnings and hence subject to the vagaries of the economy and financial markets.

Having found that the varied financial performance measures that are so often used and quoted are lacking in both formulation and application, we must consider different performance measures which may be comparable between companies.

Other external measures of performance

These include the comparison of measures of performance with other companies and organisations. As each company will vary the manner by which performance is achieved, so lessons may be learned and insights gained to improve individual company performance by such comparative studies and hence improve internal business processes. Such information about performance may be:

- informal comparisons with competitors on the basis of available published information;
- formal comparisons with competitors by means of schemes of interfirm comparisons;
- benchmarking;
- product cost comparisons.

With few exceptions, all these means of comparing performance also provide ways in which the inevitable next question can be answered – why is performance inferior to that with which the comparison is made?

Informal performance comparisons with competitors

Performance comparison with competitors on the basis of published information normally consists of ratio analysis, to allow for differing sizes of organisations. It is limited by the material available and attempts to draw the maximum from the information that can be found.

While reports and accounts are the starting point, they are limited in their usefulness, because of the variations in accounting policies that have already been mentioned, and because so many competitors will be part of diversified groups with little separate information available on the different businesses within that group. Despite these problems they will enable a view to be taken of financial structure, the performance of the company as an investment, and, with certain limitations, operating performance. Data on margins, the control of working capital and on asset utilisation will be particularly helpful.

However, this data can be supplemented from a wide range of sources:

- government and industry statistics, which may include physical measures of output, but may be available only to members of trade federations;
- EU statistics;
- for public companies far more detail than is given in the published accounts is normally given in a prospectus, which may be published because of legal requirements. Investment analysts and stockbrokers may well disclose information in their circulars that is not generally available;
- market research reports;
- credit rating agency reports such as those of Dun & Bradstreet;
- information that can be obtained by members of the company's staff in contact with suppliers and customers (selling prices, possibly price lists and discount structures, types of machinery used, materials used, numbers employed);
- there is a considerable and ever expanding range of material that can be traced through various databases and indexes (including the Internet) which can, to some extent, simplify searches. Examples may include trade press reports on investments, product launches, competitive issues, recruitment and factory expansions or redundancies.

Building up this comparative information is a slow process, and it is important to use the separate sources to cross-check each other. The consolidation of such data about competitor behaviour may provide important comparative information that may lead to establishing performance patterns that result from superior techniques and processes.

Formal comparisons with competitors

Where they exist and are available, formal intercompany schemes of comparison can be of great value. They are normally only available to participating members of trade associations. Participants provide data to a central point in confidence. This data will be about physical processes as well as financial data, and an attempt will be made to standardise data definitions, in particular accounting descriptions and analyses. The scheme operators will send back to the participant sets of ratios comparing their own performance with the industry mean or possibly with industry mean and quartiles.

The inclusion of physical data means that a much wider set of ratios can be calculated than is possible from purely financial data. The scheme operators, who are frequently independent accountants acting on behalf of a trade federation, will often assist in the interpretation of the ratios as well as in standardising the original data.

The advantages of intercompany schemes are:

- the availability of physical data to widen the range of possible ratios;
- reasonable assurance of standardised data;
- the relatively cheap preparation of comparisons with a large number of competitors;
- confidentiality.

The disadvantages are:

■ no comparison with a named and known competitor, hence no possibility of linking data gained from the intercompany scheme with other data;
■ no knowledge of adequacy of scheme coverage of industry;
■ operating schemes and preserving confidentiality becomes very difficult when there are only a few firms in an industry;
■ large, particularly multinational, firms can find that they can manage quite well without scheme data, and their non-participation can make the data worth much less to other firms. More generally, it is extremely valuable to most participants if both the largest and the most efficient firms in an industry (these are not necessarily the same firms) are members of the scheme. But membership is worth the least to these firms;
■ delays in processing tend to make the data very out of date.

Interfirm comparison schemes used to work reasonably well in industries with a significant number of competitive firms in one industry within the UK. They do not work so well when the result of rationalisation on a global scale in some industries has left only a few MNCs competing worldwide.

Governmental attitudes to trade associations, the natural sponsors and operators of these schemes, have also changed. This has been largely owing to American views of what constitutes uncompetitive behaviour, which have influenced the conduct of their subsidiaries worldwide. It may well be acceptable, even desirable, that trade associations collect data on past outputs, costs, efficiencies, prices, forecast market trends costs and output trends. But it is clearly unacceptable if the data and informal discussion provides the detail of possible future prices to particular customers or classes of customers.

Benchmarking

The objective of benchmarking is to obtain an external comparison with best practice and thus appreciate the scope for achievable improvement in efficiency. It may also be used internally when considering particular factories, branches, processes, etc., within a group of companies. Knowing what can be achieved, ideally by a respected competitor or industry leader, focuses effort on efficiency improvement, and convinces management that targets are achievable. Without this or a similar approach, operational management might not even try to achieve targets perceived to be unrealistic.

The aims of internal benchmarking can include:

■ improving performance across branches to the standard of the best branch;
■ motivating branch staff and management by demonstrating possibilities of improvement, and convincing them that the performance sought is possible;
■ using comparability to simplify and improve central control.

Benchmarking issues are not developed within this chapter but are placed for consideration with various other efficiency improvement techniques in Chapter 5. At this stage it is sufficient to state that benchmarking can be a powerful agent for improved performance.

Product cost comparison

In competitive markets, comparisons should always be made with competitor prices and competitor quotations. These comparisons are not always accurate, as potential customers of the firm can easily be tempted to provide misleading information. But they are important as they provide current information on competitiveness.

Differences in competitiveness usually imply differences in cost, but there are certain circumstances where this does not apply:

- Certain organisations may have quite different ideas about required profitability and return on investment, and it may be impossible to compete. One example of this is universities letting accommodation for conferences in vacations on a marginal cost recovery basis in direct competition with the hotel industry.
- International trade can be distorted by a production or export subsidy, by taxation or by government regulation. Thus, within the EU it is difficult to compare performance: for example, agriculture is generally subsidised in different countries, but in different ways. Establishing reliable data in these circumstances is particularly difficult, making true international comparisons problematic.
- The use of different product costing systems may lead to significant distortions. An example of this is an integrated firm using a plant-wide overhead rate, and then finding that it appeared to be very competitive for some processes, but quite uncompetitive for others. This apparent inconsistency may be eliminated by adopting activity-based costing (ABC) approaches.
- Comparison with competitor prices is available to any company which has a competitor, which is not a natural monopoly. The difficulty is in interpreting the data to be able to use it.

This data is far more important if the customer perspective is paramount than any comparison of individual processes. Simmonds (1981) linked these comparative cost ideas to the establishment of competitive advantage within the strategic management accounting literature.

Summary and a way forward

This chapter has considered various business measures which have been used to attempt to compare performance. While the financial measures have their inherent problems, they are still seen as important by both internal managers, external analysts and the financial market itself. Indeed, many are consolidated in the data sets of the better daily newspapers. The inherent problems with such financial figures is that managers may wish to improve the reported figures by data manipulation, rather than a real improvement in the business processes which are the determinants of those financial results. The other comparable performance measures which are sought to improve performance by comparison with others may lead to an accepted norm of performance rather than a search for excellence.

After considering these various performance measures, one is left with a view that comparability may be appropriate at the enterprise level, but that business performance must be viewed relative to the intentions of a particular business and its strategic direction. In doing so, the analysis of business performance has the danger of becoming insular, but if strategy is seen as 'an integrated set of actions aimed at securing a sustainable competitive advantage' (Wilson, 1991, p.82) then the external focus remains. These ideas will be further examined in Chapters 3 and 7, where change, strategic direction and performance measurement will be considered.

The financial view of business performance was put forward in the earlier part of this chapter, where various problems and issues were left unresolved. This theme will be considered further in Chapter 4, when a stakeholder perspective will be taken and particularly the notion of shareholder value analysis.

3 What You Measure is What You Get!

Introduction

This chapter will consider the relationships between corporate strategy, critical success factors and key performance indicators. The framework for the chapter will be that put forward by Booth (1998), who considers that any measurement framework should be the result of the mission, goals, objectives and strategies of the business. This chapter will consider other frameworks, particularly the *tableaux de bord* which is used by French organisations and is much more functional and departmental focused than the more project management approach of Booth. The role of specific stakeholders within the performance measurement framework will be considered in Chapter 4, as the focus of this chapter is on the internal processes rather than the broader environmental relationships of the business.

Figure 3.1: A framework for studying corporate performance measurement

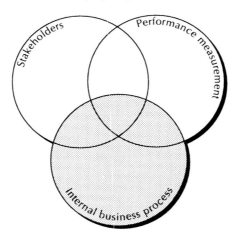

In terms of our generic framework reproduced in Figure 3.1, the focus is on the internal business processes and hence links with the issues raised in Chapter 1, where the new management agendas and challenges were presented.

Otley (1997) argues that the process of performance measurement begins with the establishment of strategic objectives and the role of the business in the extended value chain. He poses three questions which should provide focus to the above abstraction. They are, firstly, what is the business attempting to achieve and why? Secondly, how does this relate to the products and services that customers will want and be willing to pay for? Finally, what factors are crucial to the success of this venture? The answers to these questions should provide a forum for the development of a set of key performance measures that would be based on objectives and provide a view of current activities.

Otley further argues that the procedures and thinking required to answer these questions is often 'fudged'. This results in a set of performance measures which are not wholly appropriate to measure the requirements specified within the objectives. Performance measures put forward may be easy to calibrate, of minor importance or narrowly financially biased rather than broader ranging.

A framework for consideration

Booth (1997) puts forward an almost Utopian world where each employee of a business fully understands the strategic objectives, takes actions which are co-ordinated and integrated to meet those objectives and that they all have adequate feedback about the business direction and performance. This world has no place for dysfunctional behaviour, self-interest, interdepartmental rivalry and empire building. Unfortunately, this is not the case. Hence a series of measures must be inaugurated that reflect strategy while also providing a framework for control that is based on company processes and reflects the particular attributes and relationships of that business.

Booth (1998) argues that the same methods for project management can be used for organisational management. He recognises the open-ended nature of organisational management and the ongoing relationship with the environment but argues that the mutual task dependencies and scheduling of finite common resources for multiple tasks provide a strong similarity. Using this idea he puts forward the model which, in a modified form, is presented as Figure 3.2.

Figure 3.2: Measurement of programmes

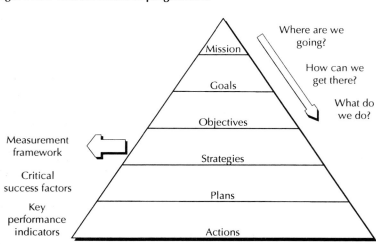

(*Adapted from:* Booth, 1998, p.27)

Figure 3.2 is very similar to a diagram put forward by Booth in 1997, where he asked a similar set of questions to those put by Otley (1997), considered earlier in this chapter.

Booth (1998) argues that performance measurement is a framework which flows from the goals and objectives of a business (or project). Other writers use the term 'vision' in place of goals and objectives. Regardless of definitional issues, there is general agreement that higher-level issues should be cascaded down the organisation.

Because Booth (1998) adopted a more contained project management framework for considering performance measurement, he avoided the problematic debate about whether a company's mission and objectives are primary to strategy (per Drucker, 1989) or subservient to strategy (per Argenti, 1989). The pyramid of Figure 3.2 clearly takes the former view. The components in the pyramid are described below.

The mission of the company is its basic function in society and is reflected in the products or services that it provides for its customers or clients (Mintzberg, 1983). Drucker (1989) argues that the mission and purpose of an organisation is required to make 'possible clear and realistic business objectives, it is the foundation for priorities, strategies, plans and work assignments. It is the starting point of the design of managerial jobs'.

Pearce and Robinson (1985) offer a list of components that a mission statement should incorporate:

- basic product/service function;
- definition of customers and markets;
- technology;
- growth and profitability;
- common philosophy;
- social responsibility and public image.

Each is a requirement which will provide clarity for the formulation of goals and objectives.

Goals are qualitative aims for the company, whose purpose is to set the criteria whereby all decisions are taken. Mintzberg (1983) described them as 'the intentions behind [the company's] decisions and actions'. They are not precise criteria for the measurement of performance.

Objectives are goals expressed in a manner by which they can be measured. They must be specific, measurable, achievable, relevant and time-bound. The traditional objective of the firm is shareholder wealth maximisation, but since the divorce of ownership and control this maxim has often been abandoned in practice. Objectives being pursued by the head of five companies in three countries as reported by Coates et al. (1993) varied in emphasis. The UK, German and US companies all considered profitability to be important. The US companies ranked growth as being more important than cash flow and financial stability. German companies ranked cash flow and financial stability quite low, but the UK companies considered these as more important objectives. Only US and German companies included environmental factors in their objectives.

Strategy is seen as how the objectives are achieved. It is operationalised in the acquisition and deployment of company assets, personnel and expertise. Managers could adopt a wide range of strategies, but any selected must position the company in relation to its environment in such a manner that will work to the pursuance of the company's objectives.

Plans are the more detailed expression of future action that reflect the goals, objectives and strategies of the business. They will include the definition and structure of specific programmes which have clear mechanisms for operation and evaluation. Actions are the manifestation of the planning processes and lead to outcomes which can be measured and evaluated.

The above process should ensure that the business remains effective by meeting its objectives (doing the right things) as opposed to being merely efficient (do things right).

The measurement framework illustrated within Figure 3.2 indicates a relationship between mission, strategy, critical success factors and key performance indicators.

Critical success factors are those attributes which drive the success of the firm, focusing on the major or primary crucial factors which will have the most impact and drive accomplishments in other supporting areas (Society of Management Accountants of Canada, SMAC, 1994). The key performance indicators are those which are useful in measuring progress (or otherwise) to strategic directions required to meet overall objectives.

Evans et al. (1996) presented the manner by which change activities at Abbey National Financial and Investment Services were co-ordinated. It is presented in summarised form in Figure 3.3.

Figure 3.3: Co-ordination of change activities at Abbey National Financial and Investment Services

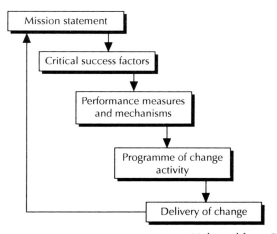

(*Adapted from:* Evans et al., 1996, p.23)

The Abbey National framework does not specify the detail of the pyramid of Figure 3.2 but it does provide the link between mission, critical success factors, performance measures and mechanisms with activities. It also highlights the manner by which performance measures and mechanisms can be used to drive change within a business's activities and the manner in which that change may lead to a revision of the mission statement.

In a similar self-learning manner, Booth (1998) has put forward an 'accountability trail', which is presented in Figure 3.4.

Figure 3.4: Accountability trail

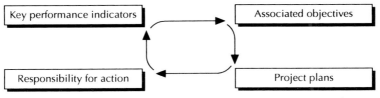

(*Source:* Booth, 1998, p.28)

The accountability trail links objectives, projected plans (which should include critical success factors) and responsibilities for actions for key performance indicators in a continuous manner. The nature of critical success factors (CSFs) will be considered prior to that of key performance indicators (KPIs).

Critical success factors

Having derived the goals, objectives and strategies of the business, it becomes possible to construct measurement frameworks which are capable of evaluating progress, and influencing progress, towards meeting those goals, etc. The term 'critical success factor' has been adopted to name those factors which drive the success of the firm.

Taking a strategic rather than performance focus, Johnson and Scholes (1997) define critical success factors as 'those aspects of strategy in which an organisation must excel to outperform competition'. They go on to say that 'CSF analysis underlines this important relationship between resources, competences and choice of strategies, which is also central to the idea of balanced scorecards for assessing performance' (p.176).

Critical success factors may include:

- quality of after-sales service;
- quality and reliability of product;
- speed to market of new products;
- speed of delivery;
- prompt payment of invoices;
- efficiency of production lines;
- flexibility of product;
- development capacity of research team;
- cross-product selling.

The above does not include an exhaustive list but does provide a listing of attributes which may be combined to give a range of CSFs that a company might recognise. The CSFs for one company may be those that are recognised and valued by their customers and suppliers.

CSFs may be classified and more easily recognised by adopting Porter's value chain analysis as a framework. Porter's model (1985) recognises five primary activities of a business, and four supporting activities, which all lead to the generation of 'margin'. Johnson and Scholes (1997) adopt this framework for an information systems supplier which is presented in Table 3.1.

Table 3.1: Linking CSFs and value chain analysis

CSFs	Inbound logistics	Operations	Outbound logistics	Marketing and sales	Service	Support activities	Managing linkages
	Underpinning competences and performance targets						
Software features	Royalty payments						Customer feedback (monthly)
Customer care		Responding to enquiries (24 hrs)			Speed of response (3 hrs)	Installations database	Customer feedback (monthly)
New business opportunities				Salesforce reports (monthly)		Competitor profiling (top 10)	Customer feedback (monthly)

(*Source:* Johnson and Scholes, 1997, p.420)

Wilson (1994) included the work of Freund (1988) who mapped the linkages between CSFs and actions for a life insurance company (Table 3.2).

Table 3.2: Critical success factors in action

CSFs	Strategies	KPIs
Ability to achieve critical mass volumes through existing brokers and agents	• Develop closer ties with agents • Telemarket to brokers • Realign agents' compensation	• Policies in force • New business written • Percentage of business with existing brokers
Be able to introduce new products within six months of industry leaders	• Underwrite strategic joint ventures • Copy leader's products • Improve underwriting skills	• Elapsed time to introduce • Percentage of products introduced within six months • Percentage of underwriters having additional certification
Be able to manage product and product line profitability	• Segment investment portfolio • Improve cost accounting • Closely manage loss ratio	• Return on portfolio segments • Actual product cost/revenue versus plan • Loss ratio relative to competitors

(*Source:* Wilson, 1994, p.23, from Freund, 1988, pp. 2/23)

The two examples quoted above provide a range of examples of CSFs for particular companies. The CSFs for any particular company will be quite specific, reflecting the strengths, weaknesses, opportunities and threats particular to that company.

Before considering key performance indicators in detail, it may be useful to consider the links between critical success factors and those indicators put forward in the *tableaux de bord* theory and practice. This framework can operate within the traditional functional hierarchical structures, with each department or subdepartment establishing its own *tableaux de bord*. This includes key performance measures for that particular part of the organisation. Hence managers in each department decide their own critical success factors which are then converted into the measurement framework of the *tableaux de bord*.

Innes (1995) argues that the development of the *tableaux de bord* for subdepartments requires considerable effort as individual managers must consider how the role of their department contributes to organisational strategy. The process is as follows:

Define objectives of the subdepartment in relation
to the strategy of the company

Decide the critical success factors of the subdepartment

Select detailed performance measures for their own
tableaux de bord

The finalised *tableaux* usually contains non-financial measures, as it is not part of the formal accounting reporting system. Lebas (1993) defined the *tableaux* as 'the managerial information system that supports the achievement of performance just like the dashboard on a car allows the driver to reach his (or her) destination…. These indicators are not all expressed in the same unit, their coherence comes from a model of the car operation system' (pp.6, 7). The *tableaux de bord* usually has several non-financial performance measures presented in chart form.

At first sight the *tableaux de bord* mechanism may mean that each subdepartment may pursue a series of individualistic objectives. This is not the case, however: each manager must integrate and co-ordinate both horizontally and vertically with other managers in the establishment of critical success factors. This results in a co-ordinated approach pursuing the same objectives and strategies. The *tableaux de bord* thus provides a 'mini' view of the link between strategy, critical success factors and key performance indicators.

Key performance indicators

Binnersley (1996) put forward the very simple proposition that performance measurement done correctly will help everybody in the company to focus on the right things, in the right place and at the right time. The ideas contained within this statement mean that performance indicators must consider criteria which includes the consideration of the:

- long term and short term;
- financial and non-financial;
- strategic aims translated into critical success factors;
- efficiency and effectiveness.

The long-term and short-term criteria linked to traditional financial measures of profitability, return on capital employed, earnings per share, etc., have already been considered in Chapter 2. They will be further developed in Chapter 4, when economic value analysis (EVA) will be developed to consider the role of the shareholder and performance measurement. The balance of financial and non-financial factors will be discussed in considerable detail in Chapter 6. This leaves two remaining issues. The first, the manner in which strategic issues are translated into critical success factors and then integrated into performance measures, will form the major thrust of this section. The second issue, that of efficiency and effectiveness, will be considered afterwards.

Examples of performance indicators put forward by SMAC (1994) include:

(i) Environmental indicators

- Hours of community service
- Hours of industry activities
- Percentage use of recyclable materials
- Amount of pollutant discharge
- Accidents and injuries resulting from products or services
- Fines/violations of government regulations

(ii) Market and customer indicators

- Share of market
- New and lost customers
- Customer satisfaction or dissatisfaction indices
- Quality performance
- Delivery performance
- Response time
- Market/channel/customer profitability
- Warranties, claims, returns

(iii) Competitor indicators

- Share of market(s)
- Customer satisfaction or dissatisfaction indices
- Quality performance
- Delivery performance
- Price performance
- New product development cycle time
- Proportion of new products
- Financial performance

(iv) Internal business processes indicators

- Product development cycle time
- Number of new products
- Manufacturing cycle time
- Inventory turns
- Order-to-delivery response time
- Sales (production) per employee
- Non-quality measures
- Reinvestment indicators
- Safety performance

(v) Human resource indicators

- Employee morale
- Applicants/acceptance ratio
- Development hours per employee
- Employee competence measures
- Employee flexibility measures
- Employee suggestions
- Turnover ratios

(vi) Financial indicators

- Revenue growth
- Market(s)/customer(s) profitability
- Product profitability
- Return on sales
- Working capital turnover
- Economic value added
- Return on capital
- Return on equity
- Cash flows

The above listings are not by any means comprehensive, but they offer a broad view of key performance indicators that provide:

- an internal and external perspective;
- a broad view of performance;
- a reflection of the human factors involved;
- a financial viewpoint; and a
- a view of the complexity of the measures.

It is important that any set of performance indicators are selected to reflect a matrix of the critical success factors that are established to meet the objectives of the business. The changes in the manner in which companies will be required to operate (as discussed in Chapter 1) will require the use of cross-team, multifunctional, performance measures that reflect cross-functional managerial processes facilitation by team working.

Figure 3.5: Process/function map for aligning performance measures

Functions / Processes	Provide service	Develop products	Sell capacity	Manage infrastructure
Marketing	• Brands value • Loyalty schemes • Responsive feedback • Customer profitability	• Customer-driven needs • Competitor benchmarks • New product design • Life-cycle renewal	• Impactful advertising • Targeted promotion • Alliance marketing • Reduced cost	
Customer service	• Warm, friendly service • Individual attention • Proactive assistance • Staff utilisation	• Staff teamwork • Service enhancement • Worldwide links • Flight efficiency		• Safe ground handling • Clean aircraft • Punctual handling • Unit cost control
Network sales	• Timely services • Value for money • Excellent connections • Distribution costs	• Route development • Alliance expansion • Customer partnering • Quality of sales	• Optimised schedules • Sales volume • Balanced prices • Negotiated agreements	
Operations	• Punctuality • Relaxing environment • Efficient processes • Unit cost control	• Facility renewal • Product development • Staff innovation • Efficient flying		• Safe operations • Improved punctuality • Aircraft utilisation • Disruption recovery
Technical services	• Reliability • Fast fault rectification • High aircraft condition • Unit cost control	• Total quality operations • Develop learning curve • 'World-class' efficiency • Future competencies		• Safe maintenance • Reduced cycle time • 'Green' operations • Make/buy decision

(*Source:* Evans et al., 1996, p.24)

Evans et al. (1996) state that 'KPIs cascade corporate goals into an accountability matrix of individual management responsibilities'. This ensures that individuals understand their team's contributions to achieving targets and the interfaces which they must manage in order to jointly succeed. Figure 3.5 provides a structure which consolidates the cascading of strategy through critical success factors into a performance measurement matrix for an airline company.

The matrix outlined in Figure 3.5 provides a linking mechanism whereby processes and functions within the business are seen to be linked through the key performance measures selected. The matrix reflects the critical success factors of the various stakeholders of the business as delegated to individual teams and departments.

The top-down process articulated in this chapter and inherent within Figure 3.5 is in conflict with that of the *tableaux de bord* process which is subdepartmental led. Regardless of origin, the essential requirement is that performance measures must be integrative and strategy based. The process to deliver a mechanism will be dependent on the contingent variables impacting on the organisation.

An approach to constructing performance measures so that they reflect a balanced approach to performance measurement is now becoming more popular. The best-known framework encapsulating this view is that of Kaplan and Norton (1992) who present a 'balanced scorecard' which includes four performance measurement perspectives. The four perspectives are:

- financial performance;
- customer knowledge;
- internal business processes;
- learning and growth.

Each attempts to consolidate the strategic issues of each perspective in key performance measures, so each of the four perspectives includes sections for key success factors and performance measurement. Rather than repeat the well-known Kaplan and Norton diagram, Figure 3.6 reproduces a balanced scorecard developed for a large hotel by Brander Brown and McDonnell (1995).

As already stated the balanced approach to performance measurement will be considered in Chapter 7.

Efficiency and effectiveness

There is a growing requirement for business operations to offer value for money (VFM). Within the public sector it is a highly debated issue, as the objectives of such enterprises are often unclear and politically motivated. Within the private sector, objectives can be specified in a much clearer manner as the societal dimension is of a smaller order of importance. However, the three Es (economy, efficiency and effectiveness) do have a part to play in the performance measures of private-sector businesses. No management team would like to argue they were anything but economic, efficient and effective!

Anthony (1965) defined management control as the 'process by which managers assume that resources are obtained and used effectively and efficiently

Figure 3.6: Balanced scorecard in the hotel sector

Innovation and learning perspective	
CSFs	*Possible measures*
New markets identified	New areas/targets identified for action
Staff development	Courses completed; internal promotions made
Improvements to facilities/services	Development areas identified; new facilities/services introduced

Customer perspective	
CSFs	*Possible measures*
Before selecting the hotel:	
Value for money	Surveys/questionnaires
Range of services offered	Surveys/questionnaires
Quality of contact/response	Third-party surveys
During stay in hotel:	
Quality of service	Guest comment cards; customer meetings
Reaction to guests' needs	Customer letters; repeat business

Internal business perspective	
CSFs	*Possible measures*
Teamwork and co-ordination	Interdepartmental meetings (reports); interdepartmental training courses
Staff development	Courses completed; number of multiskilled staff
Cost efficiency	Gross profit percentage; net profit percentage; surpluses

Financial perspective	
CSFs	*Possible measures*
Hotel profitability – both absolute and relative to the capital invested	Gross operating profit; net operating profit; return on capital employed; residual income
Sales achieved – with particular reference to sales mix and the volume/rate trade-off	Total sales; sales mix by department; sales mix by source
Management of working capital – especially of stocks and debtors	Average rate/occupancy; stock days; debtor days
Ability to react to changing markets	Areas for action identified

(*Source:* Brander Brown and McDonnell, 1995, p.10)

in the accomplishment of the organisation's goals'. The definition includes two of the three Es, and by its nature assumes the third. So how do they vary, because they are often confused and hence misstated in corporate documents?

Efficiency is concerned with the ratio of outputs relative to inputs. The ratio can be improved by reducing inputs (cost cutting) or increasing outputs (increasing volume). There are, of course, measurement problems and definition problems of both inputs and outputs. Problems of this nature have already been discussed in Chapter 2 regarding the ratio known as return on capital employed. Efficiency can be compared between processes and economic units but is difficult to evaluate in isolation.

Effectiveness is a measure of how well the objectives have been fulfilled, so linking outputs with objectives. An effective organisation is one that achieves its objectives.

Wilson and Chua (1993) maintain that organisations may be:

(i)   both efficient and effective
(ii) neither efficient nor effective
(iii) effective but not efficient, or
(iv) efficient but not effective

Lowe and Soo (1980) remarked that:

For example, if one defined effectiveness as the degree of goal achievement, then the National Aeronautics and Space Administration during the 1960s was possibly an effective but inefficient organization. President Kennedy had set a national goal of landing Americans on the moon in a decade. In 1969, after eight years of intensive research and an investment of more than 26 billion dollars, the mission was accomplished. In terms of achieving this goal, the organization was clearly effective. However, in the rush to meet deadlines and timetables, duplication was encouraged and waste inevitably occurred. But the organization was very probably not effective in the longer-run sense, since very soon after the resource flow into NASA was severely curtailed!

Since this statement was made, the spin-offs from the technological developments made during the moon programme have increased the efficiency of American industry.

Economy has a very narrow definition and is merely the less costly way of pursuing an activity. It is only input based, ignoring both outputs and objectives.

Summary

This chapter has taken a normative approach to the relationship between mission, objectives, strategy, critical success factors and performance measures. In doing so it has provided a clear framework in which managers can operate. By providing a clarity of process it may have neglected the motivational aspects required by all managers and other stakeholders. This will be addressed in the next chapter.

4 Stakeholder Perspectives of Performance Measurement

Introduction

This chapter will view the manner by which different stakeholder perspectives are considered within the overall performance measurement processes and structures. The chapter will initially introduce the concept of stakeholders from the *Corporate Report* (1975) perspective, and then select three particular stakeholder frameworks that can be used to assess performance relative to shareholders, the customers within the supply chain and the environment.

In terms of the generic framework for studying corporate performance measurement presented as Figure 4.1, this chapter focuses on the stakeholder aspect and the manner by which particular stakeholder interests are reflected in corporate performance measures. Quite a substantial part of the chapter is devoted to the shareholder as the dominant stakeholder and how these influences are being refocused in measurement techniques such as economic value added (EVA) and residual income (RI) that can be used to drive change within the internal business processes.

Figure 4.1: A framework for studying corporate performance measurement

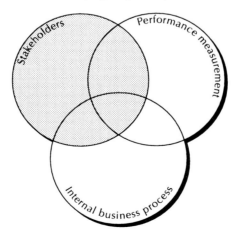

The two other stakeholders selected for particular consideration are customers and the environment, the former because of their emphasis in business processes outlined in Chapter 1 and the second because of its growing importance within the agenda of sustainable development.

The chapter will initially focus on organisational mission statements within the stakeholder concept, and then consider stakeholder power before moving into a particular consideration of shareholders, customers and the environment as major stakeholder groups. This last section will demonstrate strong links between stakeholder requirements and performance measurement.

Mission statements

Organisational mission statements are generally inclusive of a whole series of stakeholders. Consider those for BT plc, which is relatively short, and BAA plc, which is quite lengthy.

▪ *From the 1996 annual report and accounts of BT plc*

BT's mission, our central purpose, is to provide world-class telecommunications and information products and services, and to develop and exploit our networks, at home and overseas, so that we can: meet the requirements of our customers, sustain growth in the earnings of the group on behalf of our shareholders, and make a fitting contribution to the community in which we conduct our business.

▪ *From the 1996/97 annual report of BAA plc*

Our mission is to make BAA the most successful airport company in the world.

This means:

☐ Always focusing on our customers' needs and safety;
☐ Achieving continuous improvements in the costs and quality of our processes and services;
☐ Enabling our employees to give of their best.

To achieve our mission we will:

Safety and security. Give safety and security the highest priority at all times by systematically assessing and managing our safety and security risks through audited, best-practice management systems.

Employees. Provide a good and safe working environment which attracts and retains committed employees. Through training and two-way communication allow them to fulfil their potential and contribute directly to the success of the company.

Customers, suppliers and business partners. Ensure that our passengers and airlines receive excellence and good value for money in the services BAA provides and work together with our suppliers and business partners to create added value for all concerned.

Strategy. Concentrate on the core airport business, be prudently financed, continuously improve quality and cost-effectiveness, become excellent in information technology, fully develop our property and retail potential, achieve world-class standards in capital investment and develop an international business which enhances the quality and growth prospects of the Group.

Shareholders. Encourage shareholders to believe in our company by giving them consistent growth in earnings and dividends.

Environment. Recognise the concerns of the local communities, set challenging environmental targets and audit our performance against them.

Both mission statements mention customers, shareholders and the community. In addition, BAA specifically includes employees, customers, suppliers and business partners. These last four groupings are linked to the creation of value for these stakeholders through the value chain. The concept of value chain analysis (after Porter, 1985) and the critical success factors and performance measures thereto will be considered as one of the main themes of this chapter. The shareholder grouping is common to both mission statements, which is to be expected for profit-seeking companies, and these interests in performance will be considered from the viewpoint of adding value to their investment. The final theme of the chapter is the consideration of the environment. It has been included as there is currently a growing concern about pollution levels, emission controls and the recycling attributes of products. This concern will increase as various cross-national agreements on environmental issues are developed further and included within the regulatory frameworks.

Before considering these specific agendas it would be useful to reflect on the traditional stakeholder framework put forward within the Accounting Standards Steering Committee *Corporate Report* of 1975.

The *Corporate Report*

This was the result of an enquiry into the usefulness of published accounting statements. It made several proposals of which few were actually adopted, but it did summarise stakeholders and their interests in published accounting statements (see below).

User groups and their areas of interest

1. *Existing and potential shareholders*

(a) whether to buy or sell shares
(b) whether to buy a new issue of shares (e.g. a flotation or rights issue)
(c) how to vote in a takeover or merger
(d) how to vote at the annual general meeting
(e) current and future
(f) how share price has moved/will move
(g) how shares compare with alternative investments
(h) management efficiency (stewardship)
(i) future prospects (for income and capital growth)

2. Existing and potential creditors (including a lending bank)

(a) security available and the way money is used
(b) overall levels of borrowing (capital gearing)
(c) ability to meet interest payments in cash
(d) buy or sell long-term loans at the right price
(e) ability to meet loan repayment in cash

3. Employees

(a) security of employment
(b) future job prospects
(c) ability to pay wages
(d) collective bargaining power
    (i) wage settlement
    (ii) terms of employment
(e) overall performance
(f) management efficiency
(g) profits; bonuses; share schemes

4. Analysts and advisers

(a) stockbrokers – who advise investors
(b) credit rating agencies – who advise potential creditors
(c) journalists – who inform the reading public
(d) trade unionists – who advise employees

5. Business contacts

(a) suppliers – ability to pay debts; value as a long-term customer
(b) customers – deliver goods; maintain after-sales service
(c) competitors – profit margins; future developments (new operating sites, research and development, diversification); 'trade secrets'
(d) another company planning a takeover or merger – similar interest to shareholders; past record and style of operation

6. Government

(a) as a creditor
(b) as a customer
(c) as a custodian of public money and the public interest at both national and local levels
(d) contribution of company to economic well-being, employment, exports, etc.
(e) ability to pay taxes (VAT, excise duties, PAYE, NI, corporation tax, capital taxes, rates, etc.)
(f) compliance with taxation and company laws
(g) statistical information (production, sales, employment, investment, imports/exports, political and charitable donations, research, etc.)

7. The general public (taxpayers, consumers, political groups, environmentalists, etc.)

(a) role as employer
(b) role in local economy
(c) discharge of social responsibilities
(d) attitude to environmental policies
(e) contribution to national wealth

A more recent approach is that of Crockatt (1992) who put forward a sample of stakeholder expectations and related measures (Table 4.1).

Table 4.1: Sample stakeholder expectations and related measures

Stakeholder	Expectation	Measure
Employees	Good working conditions	Morale index
Shareholders	Improved shareholder value	Stock price and dividends
		Return on equity minus cost of equity
Government	Conformance to environmental regulations	Percentage of products in conformance
Customers	Product quality throughout product life	Warranty cost
	Dealer support	Number of profitable dealers

(*Source:* Crockatt, 1992)

The concept of stakeholder expectations will be addressed when the customer-related aspects of marketing performance are considered later in the chapter. The issues in Table 4.1 are very different from those in the *Corporate Report*, as the latter is concerned with an economic decision-making framework which is assumed within financial reporting. The fit between the focuses of the needs and the performance measures as presented in the annual accounts of companies has always been a contentious issue within the financial reporting literature (see, for example, Laughlin and Gray, 1988, Chapter 11). The areas of interest listed have changed in emphasis over the last 25 years. There is now greater emphasis placed on 'business contact groups' and the 'general public', the latter being consolidated in the report of the Cadbury Committee (Cadbury Report, 1992), in which companies should understand their impact on society, particularly in terms of the environment, employees and ethical issues (see Dunlop, 1998).

The themes of the 'business contact group' as viewed by the business through the marketing function and the 'environment', together with their impact on performance measures, will be developed after the issues of the main economic stakeholders, the shareholders. Before that it may be useful to consider the relative power of each stakeholder grouping.

Stakeholder power

Binnersley (1996) argued that the relative power base of each stakeholder will bias the information required by each, with the strongest influence going to the most powerful grouping, hence a predominance of measures relative to shareholders and financial analysts with a weaker emphasis on non-financial measures. The mix of stakeholders will vary with the type of business, their relative size, the industry they are in and the general environment. Johnson and Scholes (1997) offer a framework for the mapping of stakeholder relationships linking 'interest' and 'power'. They define these two attributes as follows:

- How interested each stakeholder group is to impress its expectations on the organisation's choice of strategies; and
- Whether they have the means to do so. This is concerned with the power of stakeholder groups. (p.197)

However, another view is put forward by Doyle (1994), who suggests that stakeholders generally seek satisfaction of their needs rather than their maximisation. This leads to an almost multiple constituency view of organisations where each stakeholder is willing to 'give and take' to maintain the organisation *status quo*. Binnersley (1996) illustrated the 'satisfying' of various stakeholders as follows:

- *Shareholders:* Large shareholders, generally institutional investors, prefer to sell their holdings in poorly performing companies rather than become involved in the ousting of management.
- *Managers:* Cannot be seen to be maximising their own rewards as they may be brought to account by the shareholders as acting against their interests – but this is unlikely unless excessive. More importantly, the corporate governance issues of the Greenbury Report (1995) and the establishment of remuneration committees has curtailed maximising behaviour.
- *Customers:* While these are potentially powerful stakeholders, Doyle maintains that it 'often makes substantial changes in price, quality and service relative to competitors to either attract or lose significant numbers of customers'.
- *Employees:* The power of this particular grouping is a product of the demand and supply of their particular skills in the labour market. Rather than remain in employment with a 'poor' employer in times of economic growth, they would rather move on.
- *Creditors:* This grouping has historically had the protection of legislation against unscrupulous shareholders and managers. Rather than exercise these rights through the winding-up procedures available, it is often the case that creditors will let the defaulting company continue, in the hope that it will trade itself out of its liquidity problem.

The interlinking of power and interest clearly has a major impact on the performance measures required to maintain the coalition of stakeholders. The relative movements of these variables by the different groupings will require an equal response from the business if it is to maintain the coalition. The traditional view is that shareholders are the dominant stakeholders in this coalition of interest and power, and hence it is to this grouping that we initially turn.

Shareholders

In Chapter 2 the performance measures pertinent to shareholders were mentioned but not really developed. It is the task of this section to describe and evaluate these measures, moving from the traditional accounting-based ones of profit, earnings per share and price/earnings, to the more economic and corporate finance focus of share value analysis and economic value added. This section will also illustrate how the latter measure may be used to 'drive' performance to the benefit of shareholders.

Traditional performance measurements for shareholder returns have largely been based on profit-based measures which include earnings per share and the P/E ratio. These measures are profit-derived and fail to recognise the economic value of the firm. Rappaport (1986) suggested that they were inadequate for the following reasons:

- Alternative accounting methods may be employed to measure profit;
- Risk is excluded from the measurement;
- Dividend policies are excluded;
- The time value of money is excluded;
- Investment requirements are excluded.

Some of these issues are partially answered by using a time-period-based measure of shareholder return which considers share price movements over the period (capital gain or loss) and the cash dividend received in that period. It does not address the issue of future shareholder wealth-generation through the investment in projects within the business and the future returns required to maintain shareholder loyalty.

The concept of economic value added has been developed and trade-marked by American consultants Stern Stewart, while another similar approach, cash-flow return on investment (CFROI), has been sponsored by the Boston Consulting Group. Both measures are based around the same related figures, and both attempt to provide a shareholder measure of performance that is more objective than profit and takes into account the opportunity cost of funds through a risk-adjusted cost of capital. They can be considered as the result of a series of value drivers that can be viewed to create shareholder wealth, which is taken to be a corporate objective of a company.

Economic value added

This method for the evaluation of performance has its foundations in the residual income technique where a cost of capital is charged against profit to derive residual income. At its simplest level, economic value added (EVA™) takes net operating profits after taxes less a charge for capital used to generate these profits. If EVA is positive the company has earned a greater return on the capital employed than the opportunity cost of that capital, and if EVA is negative the return on capital is not adequate to cover its capital cost. The definitions of net operating profits after tax and capital can vary depending on the basis of calculation. Regardless of approach, the profit measurement derived is closer to that of the economic profit concept. Coates et al. (1995) state that EVA has been advocated as a better measure to assess corporate performance and shareholder value creation.

There is a trade-off between the accuracy of measuring EVA and the cost of generating such a measure. While the theoretical construct of EVA is sound it is considered to be difficult to operationalise, as it either needs considerable adjustments to a traditional set of published accounts or requires financial reporting to be kept on a cash-flow basis. The Stern Stewart method of calculation is to commence with profit, rather than cash flow, and adjust it by a series of changes which attempt to remove the distortions caused by accounting methodologies. Stern Stewart recommend 160 such changes; in general, the Society of Management Accountants of Canada (SMAC) (1997) states that there are four principles that need to be followed:

1. Cash flow from operations must be established by making necessary adjustments to the reported profits. Thus, any non-cash changes to reserves or write-offs affecting both the income statement and balance sheet must be reversed.
2. Any expense that can be considered an investment for the future should be capitalised and added to the asset base.
3. The asset base must reflect the replacement value of the capital and must not be affected by goodwill or asset write-offs, so ensuring that the capital base used to calculate the change reflects the true capital employed.
4. Any adjustments made in 1–3 above must be material, visible and have an impact on managerial decision-making.

A comparison of a traditional income and a value-based income statement is presented in Table 4.2.

Table 4.2: Comparing traditional and value-based income statements

Traditional income statement	*Value-based income statement*
Revenues	Revenues
– Cost of goods sold	– Cost of goods sold
= Gross profit	= Gross profit
– Depreciation, sales, admin., other	– Depreciation, sales, admin., other
= Profit before interest and tax	= Profit before interest and tax
– Interest	– Adjusted taxes
= Profit before taxes	= Net operating profit after taxes
– Taxes	– Capital charge
= Net income	= Economic value added

(*Source:* SMAC, 1997)

In Table 4.2, the capital charge is the weighted average cost of capital multiplied by the capital base. It represents the opportunity costs of funds provided by shareholders and debt-holders. The measure implicitly includes a premium to reflect the risk attributes of current operations, and is computed after considering the tax shield on debt funds. The example below shows how the EVA for two companies can be compared for different performance attributes.

EVA example (£000)

	Company A	Company B
Revenue	900	1,500
Operating profit [a]	300	550
Adjustments for accounting measures	100	170
	200	380
Taxation on operations	100	200
'Profit' after taxation	100	180
Equity capital	300	900
Debt capital	300	100
Capital employed [b]	600	1,000
Cost of equity	15%	20%
Cost of debt after tax	9%	10%
'Profit' after taxation	100	180
Less charge for capital (W1, 2)	72	190
Economic value added	28	(10)
Return on capital employed [a] ÷ [b]	50%	55%
Profit percentage	33%	37%

W1: $600 ((^{300}/_{600} \times 15\%) + (^{300}/_{600} \times 9\%)) = 72$
W2: $1,000 ((^{900}/_{1,000} \times 20\%) + (^{100}/_{1,000} \times 10\%)) = 190$

By comparing these figures it is clear that company B is performing better by both traditional measures. It has both better profit and return on capital employed ratios. Yet when the cost of capital is deducted, company B has a negative EVA.

EVA is also associated with market added value (MVA), which will be considered after a short explanation of cash-flow return on investment (CFROI).

Cash-flow return on investment

Nichols (1998) reports that the most popular variant of this approach in the UK is where future cash flows are discounted by the weighted average cost of capital to establish either a money surplus or an internal rate of return which in turn is compared with the weighted average cost of capital. In this way the value of company performance is established, using similar techniques to those used for capital investment appraisal. Caulkin (1997) defines CFROI as a technique which compares inflation-adjusted cash flows to inflation-adjusted gross investments to fund cash-flow return on investment. While this is a slight variation, it links future cash flows to present values.

Both EVA and CFROI seek a cleaner measure of returns than the profit determined by conventional accounting principles. Hence the use of a cash, or near cash, to establish shareholder wealth, as it eliminates the problems within the profit computation.

After recognising that CFROI provides a longer-term prospective which is complex to calculate and that EVA is a simple, annually based measure, when both measures are taken together they have advantages. First, they both highlight the cost of capital and its costs. Second, by linking profits, as adjusted, with the capital base it provides a mechanism which may be used to seek opportunities for improvement. Third, attributes of shareholder value can be linked to particular internal 'value drivers'. Fourth, both techniques link into commonly used capital investment appraisal techniques, and fifth, both measures can be used to evaluate managerial performance of the economic unit.

The notion of value drivers will be explored, as it is these variables that can be used to change the performance of the business entity. So EVA is not just a measurement tool but also a mechanism whereby shareholder value creation can be generated through these value drivers.

Determinants of shareholder value creation

Any organisation must appreciate that certain performance variables drive the value of the business. Within the EVA literature they are known as 'key value drivers' but in the management accounting and strategy literature as 'critical success factors'. So factors which include customer satisfaction, manufacturing excellence, flexibility, etc., ultimately influence value. This is not a new concept, but the EVA and other measures provide a visibility to value-adding variables which profit calculations do not.

Figure 4.2 takes the four value drivers of intangibles, operating, investment and financial which ultimately lead to the creation of shareholder value by increasing cash flow of operations or reducing the cost of capital. Figure 4.3, from the same source, provides examples of this framework in using both financial and operational value drivers.

The value-creation ideas linked to EVA can be used as a mechanism whereby management decisions are focused around the creation of value. This approach is known as 'value-based management' (VBM) which monitors the performance of and takes action on the key value drivers of the business. Value is used as criteria for decision-making.

Figure 4.2: Corporate objectives and value drivers

Corporate objective	Creating shareholder value	→	Shareholder return (dividends, capital gain)

Valuation components	Cash flow from operations	Cost of capital	Cost of equity Cost of debt

Value drivers	Amount Growth rate Duration	Sales growth Profit margin Income tax rate	Working capital Fixed capital	Capital structure

Management decisions	Intangibles	Operating	Investment	Financial

(*Source:* SMAC, 1997, adapted from Rappaport, 1986)

Figure 4.3 Examples of shareholder value creation strategies

To achieve	Value drivers	Strategic requirements
An increase in cash flow from operations	Higher revenues and growth	Patent barriers to entry, niche markets, innovative products etc.
	Lower costs and income taxes	Scale economies, captive access to raw materials, higher efficiencies in processes (production, distribution, services) and labour utilisation, effective tax planning etc.
	Reduction in capital expenditure	Efficient asset acquisition and maintenance, spin-offs, higher utilisation rates of fixed assets, efficient working capital management, divesture of assets creating negative value etc.
A reduction in capital charges	Reduced business risk	Consistent and superior operating performance compared with competitors, long-term contracts, project financing etc.
	Optimise capital structure	Achieving and maintaining a capital structure that minimises the overall costs, optimises tax benefits etc.
	Reduced cost of debt	Reducing surprises (volatility of earnings), designing niche instruments etc.
	Reduced cost of equity	Consistent value creation

(*Source:* SMAC, 1997)

The VBM approach can lead to quite a change of organisational thinking and hence must be implemented with the support of senior management, using a VBM team that will provide support and education for managers who adopt it and aligning incentives to promote VBM thinking.

In this section we have moved from pure profit to the issue of shareholder performance as measured by capital growth and dividends to the more business-focused model of EVA. The latter has links into the critical success factors introduced in Chapter 3 and value-based management, which is still to be developed further.

After considering shareholders we now turn to another stakeholder, the customer.

Performance measures for marketing

There has been a greater emphasis on the customer orientation of business in the last two decades. Customers are becoming more demanding. They are also more aware of the variety of products and services on offer to them as communication channels become more sophisticated. The work of Porter (1985) in mapping the value chain within a business and the value system relating to that chain illustrates that no single organisation provides a full set of services to the customer in the creation of a product or service. There is a series of chains, as illustrated in Figure 4.4.

Figure 4.4: The value system

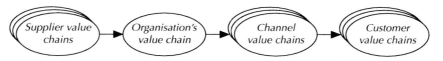

(*Source:* Adapted from Porter, 1985)

The four steps in the value system must be managed in such a manner that they provide value for the ultimate customer. Reorganising the processes that add value to the customer can be seen as a series of critical success factors relevant to the system. It is the recognition of the factors relative to the marketing function and the resulting performance measures that is the focus of this short section of the chapter.

To consider the issue from another perspective, Wright (1998), in considering the service sector, argued that in a highly competitive market the choice ultimately made by a customer in selecting a service is likely to be driven by a balance of different factors, for example, 'what managers perceive as the customer's expectation of service, the level of service offered by the competition, and management's own internal policies regarding service levels'. Although the above refers to the service sector, a similar argument can be made for product markets. Wright goes on to develop a model of performance gaps, part of which is reproduced in Figure 4.5.

Figure 4.5: Gaps relating to customers

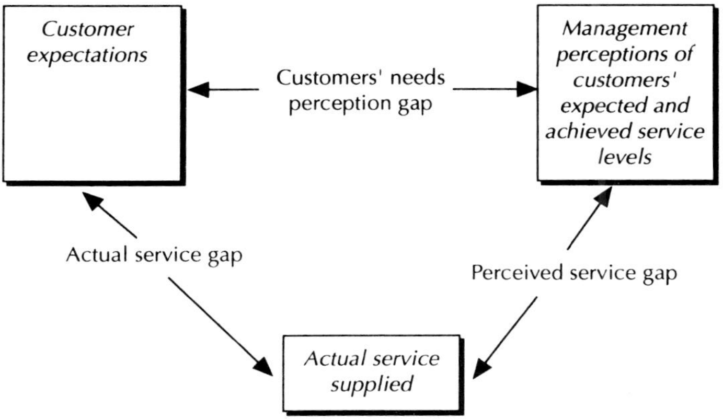

(*Source:* Adapted from Wright, 1998, p.39)

The gaps illustrated in Figure 4.5 demonstrate the need for managers to get 'nearer' to their customers, to understand their needs better and to take action that results from a series of performance measures put in place to close the various gaps. The value chain must be managed in such a manner as to maintain and enhance customer satisfaction. There are various techniques that provide mechanisms for improvement in quality and cost reductions, which include benchmarking, business process re-engineering, activity-based costing, total quality management and just-in-time techniques, all of which can be used within a policy framework of creating stronger links between the various players in the value chain. There are numerous examples of this, one of which is the market for pre-packed lunchtime snacks available in various major retail chains. Because the product has a retail shelf life of one day only, the whole value chain must operate in such a manner as to reduce the exposure to product deterioration. This requires levels of hygiene beyond those required by legislation, a sophisticated logistics network and the use of intranet communications within a framework of performance measures that are customer focused and 'flushed' through the value chain.

In a more parochial sense the marketing function of any business must view its performance on a series of dimensions after careful consideration of success factors. Wilson (1994) provides a listing of non-financial criteria which may be viewed as such. They are:

- sales value;
- market share;
- market growth;
- competitive position;
- consumer franchise;
- risk exposure;
- reliance on new products;
- customer satisfaction;
- sustainable competitive advantage.

These are much broader than the single customer satisfaction agenda and include outcomes from managerial activities as well as inputs, but they can be linked by adopting a profit impact of market strategy (PIMS) approach.

Figure 4.6: Marketing performance measure linkages

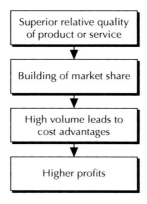

(*Source:* Wilson, 1994, p.2)

Figure 4.6 adopts an economic model that reflects additional volumes leading to additional profits. In many ways such a view is outdated, as markets are more volatile because of the rapid creation of new products and the lowering of barriers to entry which both lead to much shorter product life cycles. A business may not be able to move through the full cycle as depicted in Figure 4.6 and thus needs to be more flexible in product development, manufacture and delivery. The mechanisms that may lead to this flexibility will be considered in Chapter 5 following the section considering the environment perspective within the societal stakeholder group.

Environmental-related performance measurement

This section is very different from the previous two, and indeed different from the remainder of the book, as it attempts to consider how performance measurement related to environmental issues may evolve. After environmental issues are placed in context a model for their measurement is presented, followed by a series of speculative ideas about future performance measurements.

The Cadbury Report (1992) reported that any business should be concerned with its impact on society when it recommended a 'social audit'. This should provide a means whereby any business can understand its impact on the environment, employees and ethical issues. The task of this section is to consider the environment as a stakeholder within the performance measurement agenda. Clearly, the 'environment' is not a stakeholder in the same manner as a shareholder or creditor, but can be considered as such as the aggregate viewpoint of various environmental groups including the government, local authorities, pressure groups (including Friends of the Earth) and the general movement towards sustainable development. There are also a small number of ethical investors who are seeking to place funds with companies who are environmentally friendly.

Indirectly, insurers and loan creditors are also interested in environmental issues. Insurers may become responsible for liabilities resulting from pollution, as may loan creditors who have to 'clean up' secured assets that have fallen into their ownership by a loan default. Directly, companies may be liable for high penalties imposed by regulators for environmentally damaging behaviour. Within the supply chain, customers require a positive environmental approach within the product offering and in turn many large companies are imposing environmental responsibilities on their suppliers.

Bennett and James (1996) have identified at least six frameworks which can be used to measure environmental performance measurement. They are:

1. *Production.* This is engineering driven and is primarily a need to be more efficient with the use of raw materials and energy within the process.
2. *Environmental auditing.* As a minimum, this is carried out by companies to avoid fines, bad publicity and other problems. The criterion is compliance with regulator requirements, but proactive companies are developing mechanisms to improve their relationship with the environment.
3. *Ecological approach.* This can be value chain or site (project) related. The former considers the impact of a product or service on the environment from raw material extraction to final disposal and beyond. The latter is more focused, as it considers the use of a specific site or specific project and its impact on the environment.
4. *Quality.* This approach takes the view that there should be a continuous improvement in the performance of processes to meet environmental requirements. The emphasis is on pollution prevention rather than mitigating the impact of pollution assumed to be inherent in the production process.
5. *Accounting.* This seeks to make explicit the costs of environmental practices both for external reporting and internal management. The links between poor environmental performance and shareholder value is obvious at the extremes, but greater financial visibility of environmental issues within the firm may be harder to evaluate.
6. *Economic.* This views any process or project as one being potentially damaging to the environment, and this cost, however theoretical, should be charged as an input into any activity.

Taken separately the six approaches appear to be very different, but each is seeking an improved relationship for any business with its environment and the search for a measurement system that will make visible the costs and benefits of current and anticipated practice.

In the same article Bennett and James (1996) put forward a classification of environmental performance measures which is presented in Figure 4.7.

Figure 4.7: The environmental performance diamond

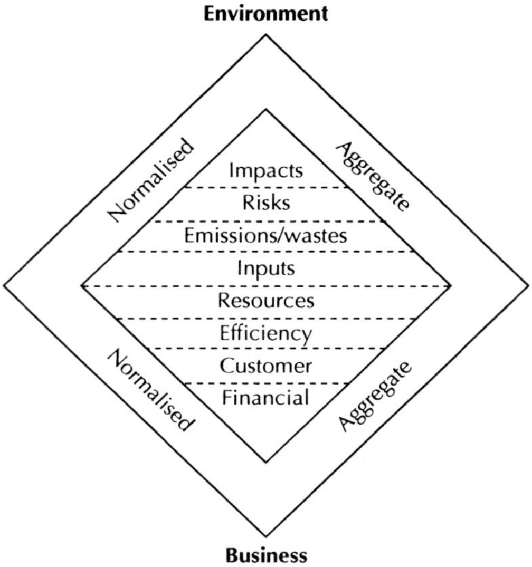

Environment

Impacts
Risks
Emissions/wastes
Inputs
Resources
Efficiency
Customer
Financial

Normalised   *Aggregate*

Normalised   *Aggregate*

Business

(*Source:* Bennett and James, 1996, p.16)

The eight measures within the diamond are ones which may be measured in a relatively simple manner. The normalised and aggregate terms that form the diamond indicate that the eight measures within can either be related to one another (normalised) or converted into different, often proxy, dimensions for aggregation. Considering each in turn:

- *Impact* measures the effect that company activities have on the environment;
- *Risk* assesses and quantifies the effect of environmentally harmful events occurring in the future;
- *Emission/waste* measures the mass or volume of actual emission made into the environment;
- *Input* and *resources* measures consider the consumption of resources used by the company in producing products or services;
- *Efficiency* measures the inputs and outputs in a manner which seeks to reduce waste outputs relative to inputs;
- *Customer* measures seek to assess customer satisfaction by the pursuance of environmentally conscious sourcing, manufacture and sale. It is seldom assessed, as it is reliant on customers' perceptions;
- *Financial* measures attempt to encapsulate environmentally related actions.

Current performance measures regarding environmental issues included by BAA in their performance indicators are as given in Table 4.3, while an earlier set of performance indicators for the UK chemical industry is presented in Table 4.4.

Table 4.3: BAA's strategic performance indicators

Noise	Infringements/aircraft movement – day
	Infringements/aircraft movement – night
	Chapter 3 aircraft in the fleet (%)
Water quality	Water supplied/pax (litres)
	Total water supplied (m³)
	Potential BOD load from de-icers (tonnes)
	Average BOD in samples, Oct–March (mg/l)
	Average oil in samples (mg/l)
Energy	Energy consumption/pax (kWh)
Waste	Waste to landfill/pax (kg)
	Waste recycled/pax (kg)
	Total waste to landfill (tonnes)
	Total waste recycled (tonnes)
Public transport	Passengers using public transport (%)
Air quality	CO_2 emissions/passenger (kg)
	Ozone-depleting potential – chemicals in stock

(*Source:* Bennett and James, 1998, p.7)

Table 4.4: Voluntary performance indicators adopted by the UK chemical industry

Health and safety	Fatalities
	Non-fatal major accidents
	Diseases
	Accidents in relation to man-hours
Environment	Amount of 'special waste'
	Discharges of 'red-list' substances
	Site-specific data expressed in an 'environmental index'
Distribution	Number of transport incidents in relation to million tonne miles
Energy	Energy consumption per tonne of product
Complaints	Number of complaints made by public and regulators

(Adapted from KPMG European Environment Briefing Note, Winter 1991/2; *source:* Gray et al., 1993)

Regardless of the focus of measurement for environmental issues, Bennett and James (1996) speculate the following:

1. environment-related performance measurement activities will continue to vary between countries and industries;
2. the more that companies use customer and financial measures to track environment-related performance, the more they will achieve good business performance and good environmental performance;
3. the more categories of environment-related performance measures a company is using, the better its environmental performance will be;

4. radical improvements in environmental performance will require the deployment of integrated – but feasible and reasonably priced – environmental information systems;

5. companies will pay increased attention in future to internal uses of environment-related performance measures and external reporting will become relatively less important; and

6. standardised meta-company approaches to environmental performance measurement are likely to be more effective than company specific.

The above may provide a highly speculative scenario but it recognises the strong link being made between environmental issues, business performance and external monitoring. Each will require a developing array of performance measurement processes, matrices and integrating frameworks.

Summary

This chapter has taken quite a broad view of the stakeholder perspectives driving company performance measurement. Each stakeholder perspective is but one view which must be aggregated and balanced among the other stakeholder perspectives. The chapter selected three particular stakeholder perspectives and considered how businesses may accommodate them within the performance measurement framework. The shareholder perspective was given greater emphasis, as this has a powerful influence on company performance issues. The customer perspective was presented in outline only, as many of the techniques involved will be developed in the next chapter where a critical resource perspective is considered and how that may be integrated into a performance measurement system. The final stakeholder perspective, the environment, is of growing importance and will become part of the developing agenda of performance measurement.

5 A Critical Resource Perspective

Introduction

Chapter 4 was concerned with the stakeholder perspective of performance measurement, focusing specifically on the shareholder perspective, a key attribute. That chapter also introduced various value-related models including economic value added (EVA™) developed by Stern Stewart. This chapter takes a different viewpoint by considering the intangible resources of the firm and how they might be enhanced through a series of modern management approaches including benchmarking, just-in-time, total quality management, business process re-engineering and activity-based management.

Figure 5.1: A framework for studying corporate performance measurement

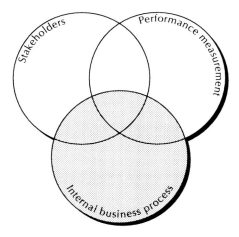

This chapter returns to the internal business processes represented in Figure 5.1. In doing so, it initially questions the simplistic application of EVA and then moves on to consider how internal processes may be improved by the use of a whole series of management techniques which enhance intellectual capital and hence performance. The particular techniques may be seen merely as individual managerial agendas, but if adopted either piecemeal or as an integrative package may enhance business processes considerably.

The first section of this chapter considers EVA and its relationship with the management process, and the second establishes an argument for the importance of intangible assets within both the value-creation capability of the firm and its impact in sustaining comparative competitive advantage. The final section outlines specific management techniques.

A reflection on economic value added and other such techniques

Regardless of the rigorous accounting adjustments recommended by the techniques to arrive at pure cash earnings, the resulting outputs for performance measurement of managerial and shareholder evaluation are subject to several flaws that may enhance or understate performance. O'Hanlon and Peasnell (1998) report that, firstly, if a business operates in a monopolistic or non-competitive market setting, even second-rate managers should be capable of generating positive EVA returns. Secondly, in some businesses past investments in competitive advantage will make it easy for current management. Equally, the EVA target may be difficult to achieve because either book asset values exceed their economic value because of general restructuring of an economy, or that project development costs are not recognised for capitalisation, so that any value added will be enhanced even though moderate returns are being generated (O'Hanlon, 1997).

The manner in which EVA is calculated may lead managers to limit capital expenditures on growth opportunities for projects, products, divisions and strategic business units because such investment would reduce the EVA figure in the initial years of the opportunity. Similarly, where strategic decisions have been made to 'harvest' a section of business then EVA may be inappropriate.

EVA is not merely a computation to establish returns: its whole approach is to empower managers to create positive EVAs by allowing them freedom to manage their business units as separate entities. It may lead managers to take a simplistic view of EVA which Mouritsen (1998) reduces to the following single rule: 'the manager has to produce and implement projects with a positive EVA, because it generates value' (p.464). In doing so it gives a simple direction for managers but assumes that managers have the ability to organise their activities to fit the EVA criteria and that they have the capabilities to devise strategies which will fulfil these criteria. EVA evaluates strategic thought *ex post* but does not provide concepts and frameworks for devising such strategies.

EVA considers individual business operations as generators of value. It does not concern itself with how that value may be generated. Its explicit recognition of tangible assets does not provide insights into the manner in which those assets are managed, or the contribution made by the intangible nature of some business assets, that are critical to the whole notion of competitive advantage and hence eventual positive EVA. A more balanced approach to performance measurement is put forward in Chapter 6, when integrated performance measurement tools are considered which do attempt to recognise the intangible nature of assets and business process by including other perspectives than the purely financial one of EVA.

The following section of this chapter considers the intangible nature of assets within the business and their strategic importance, before the final section presents various techniques which would be useful in generating positive EVA but also in recognising the intangible issues within the business process.

Intangible resources

The notion of intangible resources within a firm has long been recognised by accountants as 'goodwill'. It is usually omitted from financial statements because of their compliance with GAAP which recognises the objectivity, prudence and matching problems of recording goodwill. Nevertheless, 'goodwill' does exist within successful businesses. Hall (1993) uses the expression 'intangible resources', which include:

1. The intellectual property rights of patents, trademarks, copyright and registered designs;
2. trade secrets;
3. contracts and licences;
4. databases;
5. information in the public domain;
6. personal and organisational networks;
7. the know-how of employees, professional advisers, suppliers and distributors;
8. the reputation of products and company;
9. the culture of the organisation, e.g. the ability of the organisation to react to challenge, to cope with change, etc. (p.607)

Mouritsen (1998) uses the term 'intellectual capital' which encompasses the economy of creativity in human capital, customer capital and organisational capital and hence is less concerned with the more legalistic inclusions of Hall. Regardless of the breadth of definition, both authors take the stance that specific organisational routines, processes and mechanisms are attributed the power to generate growth (Reich, 1991) and must be recognised in both the strategic development of the company and the resulting performance measures, although there are significant problems with the latter.

Mouritsen (1998) classifies these intangibles into three sorts: human capital (which leaves the firm after hours), organisational capital (which includes procedures, manuals and administrative systems) and customer capital (customer loyalty, product brands and corporate image). The emphasis is on combined organisational capability which is gained by having the above types of intangible capital. An illustration of a capital tree is presented in Figure 5.2 and relates to the Swedish company Skandia . Within the figure the different sets of capital are put in focus with the initial split between 'financial' and 'intellectual' capital.

The measurement of intellectual capital (IC) is particularly difficult, though it is recognised as being critical to the strategic development of the firm. Its particular attributes are difficult to establish but a useful framework is put forward by Mouritsen (1998) which is reproduced as Table 5.1. The contents of this table specifies measures for 'that what is' and 'that what is done', which can be measured and related to particular departments and functions within a company. The final column, 'that what happens', has attributes which are more difficult to

Table 5.1: A template for IC measurements and representations

	That what is (statistics)	That what is done (internal key ratios)	That what happens (effect ratios)
Employees	Length of employment Formal education and training Expenses for training and education	Share employees with personal development plan Number of training days per employee Expenses for training and education per employee	Employee satisfaction Employee turnaround ratio Human resource accounting Value added per employee
Customers	Distribution of revenues on markets and products Marketing expenses	Number of customers per employee Marketing expenses per £ of revenue Administration expenses per £ of marketing expense	Customer satisfaction Share customers with long relations
Technology	IT investments Share of internal to external IT customers	PCs per employee Computer expenses per employee	IT qualifications IT licence
Processes	Expenses per process Distribution of staff on processes Investments in R&D and infrastructure	Throughput time Product-development time Time to organisationally and administratively fit new organisational units	Errors Waiting time Quality Company reputation

(*Source*: Mouritsen, 1998, p.476)

establish but are vital to the development of the firm. Kaplan and Norton (1992) presented a balanced scorecard which has one perspective entitled 'innovation and learning' which attempts to crystallise many of the elements raised in Table 5.1.

Figure 5.2: A capital tree, Skandia

The Skandia story

A firm is like a tree. Part of it is visible – its fruits – and part of it is hidden – the roots. If you only concentrate on the fruits and ignore the roots, the tree will die. For a tree to be able to grow and continue producing, one has to see to it that the roots get their nourishment.

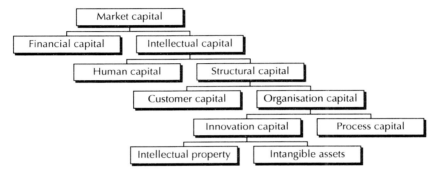

(*Source:* Mouritsen, 1998, p.476)

Hall (1993) considered the durability of intangible resources that were considered most important for business success. From a series of case studies managers considered the following to be the most durable:

▪ employee know-how;
▪ reputation;
▪ culture;
▪ networks;
▪ databases.

In the study, employee know-how was also rated as one of the most important contributors to business success as well as the most durable. Reputation was seen as so important that it must be one of the key issues for management within the general agenda of customer satisfaction requirements. Culture included various aspects: the ability to manage change, ability to innovate, ability to teamwork, high quality standards and high standards of customer service.

All the key intangible resources listed above are key attributes in the modern management techniques that form the final part of this chapter. They all have a focus on customer satisfaction through employee empowerment and group learning processes. The other key element is cost reduction, which should follow if intangible resources are encouraged to develop and are managed effectively. Each of the following techniques should improve the efficiency and effectiveness of the organisation, not by merely implementing the various procedures but by changing the thinking processes of management and workers through the development of intangible competences.

Efficiency and effectiveness techniques

The following techniques may be seen in isolation. However, the indications are that the willingness to embrace current management thinking, as witnessed by the coexistence of several approaches to performance improvement such as total quality management, business process re-engineering, activity-based costing, linked with benchmarking, shows that they can be considered as a package (Mayle et al., 1998).

Benchmarking

Mayle et al. (1998) took benchmarking to 'describe a process whereby organisations pursue enhanced performance by learning from the successful practices of others'. Comparisons may be made with other parts of the same organisation, with competitors, or with organisations operating in different spheres whose business processes are nevertheless deemed to be in some way relevant. Rank Xerox merely defines it as 'finding and implementing best practices'. The benefits and drawbacks of different benchmark partners is presented in Table 5.2.

Table 5.2: Benefits and drawbacks of different benchmark partners

Type of partner	Benefits	Drawbacks
Internal	Breaking down internal barriers; improved communication and information sharing; ease of access to partner; cost	Does not identify global 'best' practices'; internal politics/ 'turfguarding'
Competitor	As part of consortium can share costs and effort; ease of identifying partners; opening up to ideas from outside	Legal, proprietary issues
Related industry	Study of 'best practices' in generic functional or business process management; as with competitors (above)	Legal, proprietary issues; harder to identify partners
Unrelated industry	As for related industry, but may be a greater chance to discover new ideas/breakthroughs	Harder to identify appropriate partners
International	Identifies global 'best practices' as with unrelated industry (above)	Cost, time, effort; difficulty of identifying partners

(*Source:* Drew, 1997, p.429)

Regardless of partner, benchmarking considers how things are done and at what level performance is achieved. The aggregation of data about relative performance levels will not really enhance current practice, merely rank it against others. To be successful, benchmarking must lead to changing processes, procedures and activities.

Scott (1996) suggests that there is a need to develop performance profiles which identify the attributes of poor, average and excellent performance for a wide range of business processes. In such a manner, any business can use these profiles to improve current operations if they are below excellent. He goes on to suggest that business process benchmarking is important for three reasons:

1. The decision of what to benchmark can be taken as a result of critical success factor analysis. Once recognised, the business processes at which the company must excel are visible for benchmarking.
2. For benchmarking to be successful an acceptable degree of comparability is required. This is usually gained through process comparisons rather than functional comparisons.
3. Benchmarking complements the focus of business process re-engineering and should be taken together (this link will be explored later in the chapter).

Benchmarking requires a close analysis of current practice within the focal organisation before any sensible comparisons with others can be made. This analysis means that any change triggered by benchmarking can be implemented with full regard to the systems and processes currently in operation. Scott (1996) argues that the benchmarking of soft processes like 'organisational learning, developing personal contributions, and so on' should be included, as they may help managers and others understand the changes needed when hard processes such as 'logistics, order fulfilment, distribution and the like' are part of the change processes.

Drew (1997) argues that benchmarking will vary with the nature of the object being benchmarked and the partners with whom comparisons are being made. Benchmarking may be classified into various categories, which may not be exclusive. Drew uses the following:

- Process benchmarking used to compare operations, work practices and business processes;
- Product/service benchmarking used to compare product/service offerings;
- Strategic benchmarking used to compare organisational structures, management practices and business strategies.

The Society of Management Accountants of Canada uses a slightly different set of categories which are based on what is being measured and who is being benchmarked. The former is illustrated in Figure 5.3.

Figure 5.3: Types of benchmarks based upon what is being measured

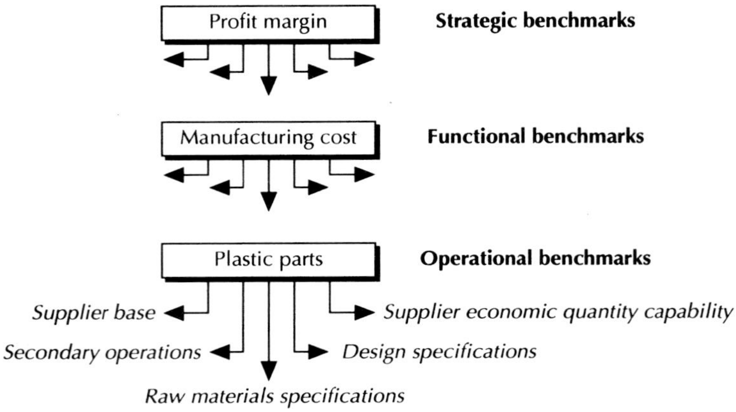

| Profit margin | **Strategic benchmarks** |

| Manufacturing cost | **Functional benchmarks** |

| Plastic parts | **Operational benchmarks** |

Supplier base ◄── ──► Supplier economic quantity capability

Secondary operations ◄── ──► Design specifications

Raw materials specifications

(*Source:* SMAC, 1993a)

The latter is classified as:

(a) competitive benchmarks;
(b) internal benchmarks; and
(c) analogous benchmarks

Regardless of category, benchmarking must be seen within a process of change management which can be summarised in the framework illustrated in Figure 5.4.

While each phase is important if benchmarking is to move beyond the mere ranking at the 'implementation/execution' stage, action must be taken by the focal organisation if real improvement is to be developed and consolidated. For successful benchmarking to be undertaken and the results of it implemented, it requires the sponsorship of very senior managers and a willingness by his or her subordinates to participate in the enquiry and the subsequent management of change. Benchmarking can be a valuable tool for introducing improvements, but such a process requires the willingness of all levels of management and subordinates to adapt and learn from others. The capacity to learn and translate that learning into positive action may require substantial empowerment of workers and a move away from 'command and control' management styles.

There is no doubt that benchmarking can be used to improve performance, but it should not be relied upon to create competitive advantage as it may merely bring performance up to best in class rather than making a breakthrough in technological leadership, marketing initiatives or cost advantage. However, benchmarking will improve the performance of individual companies within a sector, so driving the innovative ones to seek further competitive advantages.

Figure 5.4: The five phases of benchmarking

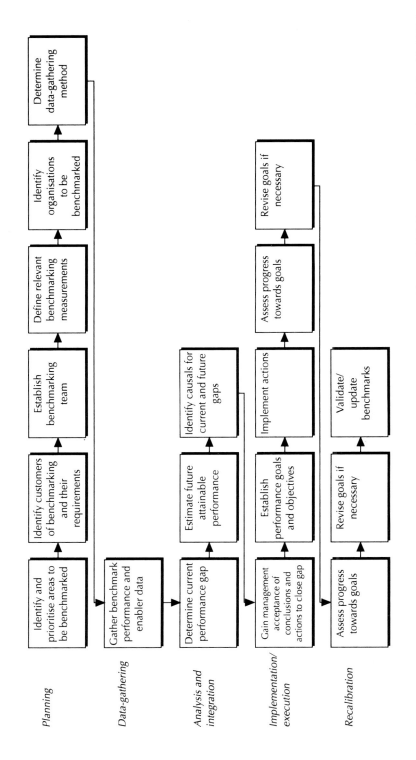

(*Source*: SMAC, Management Accounting Guideline 16, 1993a)

Just-in-time

CIMA (1996) defines just-in-time (JIT) as 'a system whose objective is to produce or to procure products or components as they are required by a customer or for use, rather than for stock. A JIT system is a 'pull' system, which responds to demand, in contrast to a 'push' system in which stocks act as buffers between the different elements of the system, such as purchasing, production and sales' (p.29).

The JIT approach is outlined in Figure 5.5 which demonstrates the customer initiating activity by requesting the supply of goods which will be responded to by the supplier initiating activity to meet that request. Supplies would have to be ordered and made available as the first production phase required them. The goods would be produced, moving through the plant in a smooth manner without undue delays, to be dispatched to the customer. For this to be achieved good communications must exist with suppliers and supply reliability must be ensured. This may require delivery of supplies daily or even hourly, which may result in suppliers clustering around major factories using the JIT system.

Figure 5.5: The JIT concept

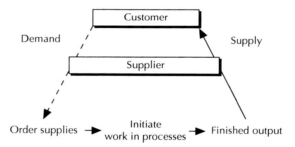

(*Source:* Tanaka et al., 1993)

The above definitional description of JIT suggests that it is merely procedural, which will be financially attractive through the reduction of inventory costs and the opportunity costs of the funds committed to those stock holdings. This procedural approach to JIT may be beneficial, but JIT can be considered to be a whole philosophy if adopted in full.

JIT is a philosophy of continuous improvement in which non-value-added activities are identified and removed for the purpose of reducing costs, improving quality, performance, delivery and flexibility. To achieve this, management and subordinates must have a commitment to continuous improvement and the pursuit of excellence in the design and operation of the production management system.

The Society of Management Accountants of Canada (1993b) mention that JIT can be applied to all parts of an organisation, but provide a list of twelve programmes or projects that are applicable to JIT manufacturing:

(i)   improve communications;
(ii)   improve quality;
(iii)   improve equipment reliability and capability;
(iv)   improve workplace organisation;
(v)   train employees and upgrade their skills;
(vi)   modify control systems to support JIT;
(vii)   reduce set-up times;
(viii) train multiskilled employees;
(ix)   develop a pull control system and do value-added analysis;
(x)   integrate suppliers;
(xi)   improve product design and design processes;
(xii)   improve layout.

Each of the above will be considered using extracts from the SMAC Management Accounting Guideline 19, which is more fully reproduced in Scarlett (1997).

(i) Improve communications

Employees are prepared for the changes that will take place by being given information in advance and by receiving training. Personnel receive information about projected changes and the reasons why they are necessary. The communication goals are to gain support for the changes and have employees participate in the change process.

(ii) Improve quality

Quality is assessed at each production operation and at each support operation. Total quality management (TQM) is used to maintain and improve the level of quality in all activities throughout the organisation. Responsibility for quality is transferred from inspectors to operators. Quality is 'built in' rather than 'inspected in'. These issues are considered more fully under the title TQM later in this chapter.

(iii) Improve equipment reliability and capability

After the quality improvement project is started, work on improving the reliability of production equipment usually begins. A cross-functional team, consisting of personnel from production, maintenance, tooling, materials, engineering, etc., is formed for each product. The team studies each operation that is required to manufacture the product, and seeks answers to questions ranging from the basic, 'Is the operation needed?', to the more applied, 'Can operators do simple continuous maintenance?'

(iv) Improve workplace organisation

In a JIT production system, material moves through the factory very quickly in response to signals from the pull control system. All of this requires the factory to be very well organised. JIT also requires fast set-ups, which can only be done when tools and fixtures are well organised. Good quality requires that floors, equipment and work areas be clean and tidy. When the factory floor is well organised and clean, problems become visible. Steps can then be taken to solve the problems.

(v) Train employees and upgrade their skills

Personnel are provided with skills to participate in the implementation of the JIT production system and to do the new jobs in JIT. Training provides employees with these new skills. Once operators have received training in quality improvement, equipment improvement, etc., training is extended to other employees in other areas, the amount varying according to their needs. Some employees are trained to be the trainers of other employees.

(vi) Modify control systems to support JIT

This project primarily affects the structure and controls area of the current production system, which must be reviewed to determine whether they are appropriate for a JIT production system as opposed to a craft or mass-production system. The system for measuring performance is also changed. Traditional measures such as equipment use, efficiency, direct and indirect labour ratios, overhead ratios, set-up to run-time ratios and so on are less useful in a JIT production system. For example, equipment usage is not an appropriate performance measure as it is preferred to have equipment idle rather than producing for stock. JIT seeks to eliminate all non-value-added activity regardless of where it occurs, so JIT performance measures are best expressed as tracking actual cost reductions, improved quality, reductions in delivery time and the like.

(vii) Reduce set-up times

A JIT production system requires the ability to produce quickly in small lots. This cannot be done if set-up times are long, hence the need to reduce these times. To achieve such reductions it may be necessary to improve equipment, tools, fixtures, work methods and employee skills. Such improvements should also result in improved quality, lower cycle times and fewer breakdowns.

(viii) Train multiskilled employees

Multiskilled employees are required in order to achieve the flexibility required to respond quickly to changes in demand and product mix. Operators may be required to move to different areas, machines or functions. This requires job descriptions which are broad and that ensure that operators are able to perform many different tasks. These skills help the JIT production system to increase its levels of quality, performance, flexibility, and innovativeness, while reducing cost and delivery time.

The compensation system used in a JIT production system pays employees for the number of different jobs they have mastered, rather than for the job they happen to be doing. At the same time, the number of different job classifications in a JIT production system is less than for the other production systems.

(ix) Develop the pull control system and do value-added analysis

This project primarily affects the production planning and control system area of the current production system. While there are several ways that the pull control system can be organised, the best known is the *kanban* method. A kanban is a signal that a production requirement exists. There are many kinds of kanban – electronic kanban, one-card kanban, dual-card kanban, triangular kanban, etc. Each of these kanbans is:

- A container of standard size in which a fixed number of units of a product is placed; and
- A card that controls the use of the container and its contents.

Production kanbans authorise the production of more products. They are placed at the points where the products they contain are produced. Move kanbans authorise the movement of material from one location to another. They are placed at the points where the products they contain are used. When all the products in a move kanban container are used, the empty kanban is moved to the point where those products are produced. Units are transferred from the production kanban to the empty move kanban, after which the move kanban is returned to the point where the products are used. If a production kanban is emptied during this process, a replenishment is triggered to produce just enough units to fill the empty production kanban. The movement of kanbans and triggering of production replenish empty production kanbans comprise the pull control system.

JIT divides all activities into two categories, those which add value and those which do not. The elimination of the latter will reduce costs. Common areas for elimination are overstocking, producing defective parts, producing inefficiently, waiting, transporting products unnecessarily and moving staff unnecessarily.

(x) Integrate suppliers

Because raw material and semi-finished inputs are a significant part of the final cost of the product, it is necessary to link suppliers into the production system. The objective is to find the best supplier by using a cross-functional evaluation team which will consider issues ranging from the supplier's financial strength to its capability for continuous improvement and price. A supplier is sought which will best fit with the JIT processes employed by the user company, so that quality and delivery become important inputs into the selection of suppliers.

Once selected, a formalised relationship is established which will at the lowest level require minimum standards of performance but at the higher levels may lead to regular liaison meetings, the joint design of products and the general development of the supplier's capabilities to contribute. This aspect will be considered further in Chapter 7 within value chain analysis.

(xi) Improve product design and design processes

Quality problems may result from inadequate design, which may lead to production difficulties and products being rejected. Again, a cross-functional team is charged with the task of studying current products, the desire being to make improvements. This usually leads to the development of modular designs with standard parts to simplify manufacture and improve quality. The team would consider the manufacturing processes needed for specific designs and thus seek reduced production times within the design stage.

(xii) Improve layout

A team is charged with studying the material flow and the equipment layout to determine where improvements can be made. It may, for example, be possible to relocate equipment into focused manufacturing cells.

All the above projects will lead to a greater understanding of the current production system, its supplier links and its quality. In doing so, improvements can be sought that not only provide just-in-time delivery of parts but the entire philosophy of JIT which seeks continuous improvement in quality and an assumed reduction in cost.

TQM and BPR in context

The next section of this chapter considers two quality improvement techniques and philosophies: total quality management (TQM) and business process re-engineering (BPR). They both deal with quality issues, though in different ways, and may often complement each other.

TQM takes the view that the processes of production and service generation within the firm are basically sound but can always be improved by the continuous evaluation of those processes by empowered employees. In contrast, BPR involves a significant step change: it is concerned with radical changes to the processes, people and information systems within one step change. It is not incremental and is designed to improve performance quickly rather than incrementally through TQM. It may be that TQM would naturally follow a BPR initiative. The distinction between BPR and TQM is provided in Figure 5.6, while Fitzgerald et al. (1998) put forward the characteristics of radical versus continuous improvement strategies which is presented in Figure 5.7.

Figure 5.6: Degree of change and pace of change

		Pace of change	
		Fast	*Measured*
Degree of change	*Tactical*	Focused improvement	Continuous improvement (TQM)
	Radical	Business process re-engineering (BPR)	Business process innovation

(*Source:* Institute of Internal Auditors, 1996)

Figure 5.7: Characteristics of radical v. continuous improvement strategies

Aspect	STRATEGY	
	Radical change	**Continuous improvement**
Basic characteristic	Short term, big step change	Long term, small step change
Time period	Intermittent and non-incremental	Continuous and incremental
Type of change	Abrupt and volatile	Gradual and constant
Employee involvement	Champions selected, typically high-level executives	Everybody
Approach	Individualistic	Collectivist (team-based)
Stimulus	Technological breakthroughs, new inventions, methods and theories	Conventional know-how and state-of-the-art
Decision-making	Top down	Bottom up
Focus	Results, predominantly financial	Culture change
Risks	Concentrated	Distributed
Costs	Large investment, technology focused, short-term results	Small investment, people and process focused, long-term results

(*Source:* Fitzgerald et al., 1998)

While Fitzgerald et al. distinguish between the two improvement strategies, they conclude their paper by stating that the strategies are 'very similar in terms of their characteristics and appear simply by degrees ... they are almost shadows of one another'. They also reported that 82 per cent of the sample of continuous improvement programmes and 74 per cent of radical change programmes were considered to be successful, which is a higher proportion than previous studies.

Total quality management (TQM)

To put TQM in context, Dale et al. (1990) suggests that there is a continuum of quality management approaches which is at its highest functional level in TQM. The progression through the four stages is illustrated in Figure 5.8.

Figure 5.8: Quality management

(*Adapted from:* Dale et al., 1990)

The lowest level of quality management system is quality inspection, whereby the products are examined, measured and tested to specified standards. It should take place at appropriate points within the production cycle, usually by specialist staff who will assess if faulty goods can be scrapped, reworked or sold as substandard. The next step, quality control, is similar to quality inspection but involves self-inspection by operatives to take place. Both inspection and control involve the *ex post* evaluation of quality by individuals, but the next step in the management of quality requires a change in emphasis away from the detection of errors to the prevention of errors.

Quality assurance provides a series of mechanisms that provide confidence that a product or service will satisfy the specified attributes of quality. The assurance process may require statistical process control, quality audits, quality manuals and other mechanisms that should provide *ex ante* mechanisms for ensuring quality. The final stage of the quality management hierarchy is TQM.

Bromwich and Bhimani (1994) state that 'TQM requires the principles of quality management to be applied in every branch and at all levels of the organisation including not just products and services provided but also sales, finance, personnel and other enterprise activities. The process may also extend beyond the organisation itself to provide partnerships with suppliers and customers' (p.33). Scarlett (1997) maintains that 'TQM is a culture of continuous improvement ... this culture postulates that workers are the experts because they know how the work is done' (p.71). Bringing these two themes together means that TQM should embrace all the activities within the organisation and is worker focused, so moving away from a top-down 'command and control' philosophy of management. This represents a significant shift of thinking from traditional control measures and their performance measurement approaches. It requires the reduction of functional boundaries and the recognition of a long-term process of quality improvements. Ultimately, TQM should reduce costs and ensure customer satisfaction.

Babicky (1996) argues that the TQM philosophy has the basic underlying belief in the capability and desire of each and every worker to make good decisions, contribute ideas that support efficiency, and make a place where they can enjoy working together. This is a great step away from traditional management philosophies which rely on performance measures based on control and exemption reporting to ensure that workers are complying with management-dictated norms.

Customer service is the focus of TQM, but requires several basic components for its implementation: employee empowerment, continuous improvement, measurement and strong leadership.

The empowerment of employees is a basic component of TQM. It means that employees should have the authority and the responsibility to take and implement decisions that are in the best interests of the organisation. This should lead to job enrichment and improvement. The TQM philosophy considers that the best individuals to improve the work and quality of the product are those closest to it, as they understand the process and can see incremental improvements. This again moves the management of activities to the workforce, as management teams seeking efficiencies are no longer required.

The never-ending process of continual improvement should become part of the organisation's culture. Hence, an atmosphere of seeking and implementing improvements must be sought that is worker centred. The old maxims of standardisation, streamlining and simplification still apply but are now worker focused within a culture of continuous improvement.

The measurement of the elements of a quality organisation is often difficult as many of its facets relate to human resources, culture and the environment. Regardless of this, however, a strong information system is required to recognise and measure the key performance indicators indicated by critical factor analysis. It is the measurement of performance that gives reassurance of the individual quality-focused improvements generated by individual workers.

Strong leadership must be exercised if TQM is to be implemented. The process of change to a TQM culture may not be carried out quietly. The leadership and implementation through cross-functional and multi-hierarchical teams will require the sponsorship and ownership of senior managers to sustain its development over quite lengthy periods of time. Once attached, the customer-focus emphasis should provide employees with a sense of inclusion where products and service offerings have all the attributes of quality required by the customers. Such a process will require a process of communication, education and support throughout the organisation.

There is evidence to suggest the TQM, once established, is successful but may require several accounting reporting periods to be seen in bottom-line profit improvement. While the philosophy of TQM may be grand, the ultimate objective is to increase relative competitive advantage through improved quality and reduced costs.

Business process re-engineering

We have seen that BPR involves quite a considerable quantum step change in the manner in which an organisation operates, which contrasts with the incremental approaches of TQM. The process of BPR can be described as revolutionary not evolutionary, as it changes the way work is performed to gain significant improvements in quality, speed of operation and cost savings. While BPR maintains the customer as the key beneficiary of change, it involves significant aspects of manpower, technologies and business processes.

BPR cuts to the base of the business process by asking very simple questions about where, when, by whom and not just how, work is performed. It also considers the interdependencies of the answers to those questions. Figure 5.9 illustrates the constituent elements of a successful BPR process.

Figure 5.9: Elements of the BPR process

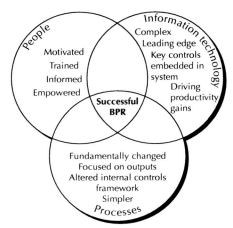

(Source: Institute of Internal Auditors, 1996)

The trigger for BPR is often when competitive forces have created an opportunity or where a radical revamp is necessary to maintain competitive positioning in the marketplace. Hence BPR may be reactive or proactive, but should have the following long-term benefits:

▪ the organisation should become customer focused to meet their satisfaction;
▪ line managers will be given greater responsibility and hence should improve control aspects;
▪ the process-based nature of employees' roles should provide greater flexibility;
▪ a full review of activities should mean that the supporting information technology reflects user needs;
▪ these actions should lead to cost reductions by reduced manpower levels, and better management of resources which should lead to productivity gains.

BPR also streamlines processes with the elimination of non-value-added work, through the analysis of each activity and its contribution to profitability.

Clearly, the improvements put forward above will have significant implications for management, employees, technology, customers and suppliers. The process is likely to be expensive in terms of management time, internal disruption and staff morale, but should provide an improved set of processes after completion.

Activity-based approaches to costing and management

Activity-based costing (ABC) was the first real development in the activity-based management area. It is concerned with the need to make more realistic allocations of overhead costs to products. It emphasises the requirement to obtain a better understanding of the behaviour of overhead costs, and thus ascertain what causes overhead costs and how they relate to products. Cooper and Kaplan (1988) argue that activity-based costing techniques address the real issues of how and why overheads are being spent. The concept is that managers can only manage costs by managing the activities that cause the costs (Figure 5.10), hence activity-based management (ABM).

Figure 5.10: An outline of the activity-based costing system

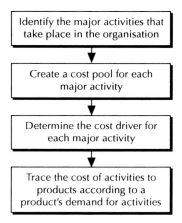

(Source: Broadbent and Cullen, 1997)

Innes and Mitchell (1990) provide a neat summary of the benefits and limitations of activity-based costing:

Benefits

- Provides more accurate product line costings, particularly where non-volume-related overheads are significant and a diverse product line is manufactured.
- Is flexible enough to analyse costs by cost objects other than products such as processes, areas of managerial responsibility and customers.
- Provides a reliable indication of long-run variable product costs which is particularly relevant to managerial decision-making at a strategic level.
- Provides meaningful financial (periodic cost driver rates) and non-financial (period cost driver volumes) measures which are relevant for cost management and performance assessment at an operational level.
- Aids identification and understanding of cost behaviour and thus has the potential to improve cost estimation.
- Provides a more logical, acceptable and comprehensible basis for costing work.

Limitations

- Little evidence to date that ABC improves corporate profitability.
- Little is known about the potential behavioural, organisational and economic consequences of adopting ABC.
- ABC information is historic and internally oriented and therefore lacks direct relevance for future strategic decisions.

- Practical problems such as cost driver selection and cost commonalities are unresolved.
- Its novelty is questionable; it may be viewed as simply a rigorous application of conventional costing procedures.

While the Innes and Mitchell study provides a sound analysis of ABC, it is worth considering the practice within lean enterprises. Cooper (1996b) defines such an organisation as one that adopts JIT, TQM, team-based arrangements and supportive supplier relations, which all move towards improved customer satisfaction. He considers that ABC would generally lead to larger batch sizes, which would run counter to the JIT philosophy. This may be the case but, because of the visibility of the activities which drive costs, management is in a better position to balance the batch size issue. In a similar manner, an ABC system would recognise the costs of defective production and hence lead to the avoidance of such defects, so improving quality.

Roberts and Silvester (1996) compared ABC and ABM as follows, recognising that ABC and ABM terms may be used interchangeably. Strictly speaking, however, ABC refers only to the actual technique for determining the costs of activities and the outputs that those activities produce. Although no technique can produce perfect cost estimates, the aim of ABC is to generate improved cost data for use in managing a company's activities.

ABM is a much broader concept. It refers to the fundamental management philosophy that focuses on the planning, execution and measurement of activities as the key to competitive advantage. Viewed from this perspective, an ABC implementation failure could be defined as the inability of a company to move from simply generating ABC information towards actually using the information to improve profits.

Because activity-based costing explicitly identifies activities which drive costs, these activities can become the focus of management action. If these activities can be improved and streamlined then their associated costs can also be reduced. There has been much criticism of ABC and its ability to produce 'better' product cost information, but this same system has led to a recognition by management of which activities require special attention. By identifying the underlying drivers of all activities, ABM provides an understanding of the resource implications of various causes of action by identifying value-adding and non-value-adding activities.

A particular customer-focused approach of ABM is the approach to customer profitability analysis. Much has been said in this and other chapters about customer orientation but little has been made of customer profitability. Traditional accounting objections to this method are those levelled against ABC itself, including cross-functional activities, blurring responsibility, profit centre rather than individual customer accounting, and the unwilling recognition that customer service is just part of the customer offering.

Customer profit analysis (CPA) demands that all costs relevant to the trading relationship with a particular customer should be considered. As suppliers and customers move together within the supply chain, the recognition of particular provided services must be quantified. The following specialist services may be provided for a particular customer in addition to the normal: quality control, merchandising, retrospective discounts, promotions, financing costs, technical query support, and so on.. The cost of these particular services will be additional to the normal volume-based costs of bulk delivery compared with small-lot delivery.

As customers vary in their particular requirements, so profitability can also vary between them. CPA requires the establishment of profitability levels for each customer; this is done by analysing the purchased product or service portfolio for each customer and the consideration of all support activities for each customer. Once established, individual customer profitability statements can lead to a review of the relationship, not to put up prices, but to provide the same service through leaner supplier support relationships.

Summary

The chapter commenced with a short critique of EVA™ which demonstrated the lack of intangible considerations within that formulation. It then developed the importance of intangible resources within the need to enhance competitive advantage, and presented a matrix that may provide a performance measurement framework for such intangibles. The latter part of the chapter introduced a series of management techniques that are procedural to enhance efficiency but which also include the agendas of building intangible competences within the organisation to enhance effectiveness. The intangible competences include empowerment of employees, value-added activity analysis, cultural issues of quality improvement, benchmarking and other staff developmental activities, including the ability to work in cross-functional groups to provide proactive, flexible management mechanisms.

6 Integrated Performance Measurement Tools: A Balanced Approach

Introduction

Johnson and Kaplan (1987) refer to the practice of 'managing by numbers' by which organisational, operational, managerial and strategic issues are reduced to mere accounting numeric expressions of performance measurement. As already argued in Chapter 1, the changing nature of business has meant that performance measurement has needed review in order that issues of quality, customer satisfaction, competitive positioning and flexibility, which are inherent within ideas of competitive advantage and strategic choice, can be aggregated into performance measurement. Performance measures must provide a mechanism whereby determinants of performance are evaluated in parallel with, and prior to, the measurement of results. This view is compatible with the ideas of strategic management accounting (Simmonds, 1981) where aggregate financial performance, as measured by annual accounting profit, is merely a residual from the determinants which contributed to enhancing and maintaining competitive advantage. This view is also compatible with those concerned with the management and measurement of 'upstream' activities prior to manufacture that will eventually compound into 'downstream' activities and ultimate performance. Hence there is a need to provide a framework which measures both the determinants and the results of organisational performance.

This chapter brings together several themes that have been developing within the previous chapters and provides a series of frameworks for performance measurement which would sit in that element of the framework put forward in Figure 6.1.

Figure 6.1: A framework for studying corporate performance measurement

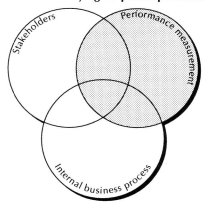

Performance measurement systems

Euske et al. (1993) classified performance measurement systems into four types:

- financial orientation;
- financially constrained but improvement focused;
- balanced or blended;
- 'swing' or rotational.

The first three exhibit a continuum that moves from the heavy reliance on financial metrics (Johnson and Kaplan, 1987) to one where there is a need to balance or blend various financial and non-financial performance measures. The fourth classification is where performance measurement systems appear to differ from year to year in an attempt to reflect the changing variables affecting the organisation.

There has also been movement from the strictly financial performance content to the more balanced view of performance measurement which considers determinants as well as results. This theme will be continued within this chapter when the balanced scorecard (Kaplan and Norton, 1992) and the results and determinants framework (Brignall et al., 1991) will be considered. In preparation, it would be useful to consider the focus of control and performance measurement.

Focus of control and performance measurement

McNair et al. (1990) argued that performance measures must be tailored to suit the goals and aspirations of different levels of an organisational hierarchy. Measurement of physical and operational issues will be greatest at the lower levels within the hierarchy, while economic and financial measurement will be more important at higher levels. This is demonstrated in the performance pyramid reproduced in Figure 6.2.

Figure 6.2: The performance pyramid

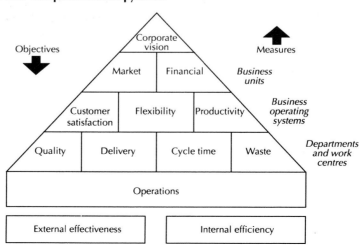

(*Source:* McNair et al., 1990, p.30)

Management accounting textbooks concur with the view put forward by McNair et al. in that different performance measures provide feedback and learning cycles for different levels of the organisation, and that only summarised measures are released to the next, higher level of management. Managers operating between upper and lower levels within the hierarchy select and convert performance measurements into those relevant and meaningful to both upper- and lower-level managers. Hence, financial goals established by corporate managers are translated into defined operational goals for operational managers. As organisations incorporate new management practices to become more flexible and reflective about the changing environment in which they operate, then a more balanced view of organisational goals and performance measurement is required to facilitate the development and implementation of strategic thinking which links operational performances with strategic objectives. Two such frameworks are considered below.

A balanced view of organisational performance

We have seen the balanced view of performance measurement as part of a typology of measurement systems (Euske et al., 1993) as a way of integrating organisational objectives. Two particular frameworks incorporating this balanced view will be presented, those of Kaplan and Norton (1992) and Brignall et al. (1991). Both have common themes and attributes, although the former has a manufacturing focus while the latter has a service industry focus. Both frameworks attempt to provide not only diagnostic measures of performance but also a strategic focus which integrates the aspirations of the organisation into a single 'card' or 'framework'.

Kaplan and Norton (1992) argue that managers should not have to choose between financial and operational performance measures, but should be provided with a comprehensive overview of the business. Their balanced scorecard includes financial measures that highlight the results of actions already taken. These financial measures are then complemented with a series of operational measures from which that financial performance is derived. The operational measures put forward by Kaplan and Norton have the following focuses (Figure 6.3):

- financial perspective;
- customer perspective;
- internal business perspective;
- innovation and learning perspective.

Figure 6.3: The balanced scorecard for Electronic Circuits Inc.

Financial perspective	
Goals	*Measures*
Survive	Cash flow
Succeed	Quarterly sales growth and operating income by division
Prosper	Increased market share and ROE

Customer perspective	
Goals	*Measures*
New products	Percentage of sales from new products; percentage of sales from proprietary products
Responsive supply	On-time delivery (defined by customer)
Preferred supplier	Share of key accounts purchases Ranking by key accounts
Customer partnership	Number of co-operative engineering efforts

Internal business perspective	
Goals	*Measures*
Technology capability	Manufacturing geometry v. competition
M'facturing excellence	Cycle time; unit cost; yield
Design productivity	Silicon efficiency; engineering efficiency
New product introduction	Actual introduction: schedule v. plan

Innovation and learning perspective	
Goals	*Measures*
Technology leadership	Time to develop next generation
M'facturing learning	Process time to maturity
Product focus	Percentage of products equalling 80 per cent of sales
Time to market	New product introduction v. competition

(*Source:* Kaplan and Norton, 1992, p.76)

The scorecard of Figure 6.3 demonstrates the manner in which each attribute of performance is composed of two elements. The 'goals' are derived from organisational strategy and the 'measures' are employed to measure the performance of that particular 'goal'. This mechanism should assist in the manner by which strategic thinking is communicated throughout the organisation, as managers can relate their activities to the scorecard. The very visible manner in which the scorecard is presented will assist managers operating between upper and lower levels within the hierarchy (after McNair et al., 1990) in selecting more appropriate performance measures to be delegated downwards and aggregated upwards.

The Brignall et al. (1991) framework (Figure 6.4) is titled the 'results and determinants framework', so linking the theme of goals and measures put forward by Kaplan and Norton. However, the results focus is somewhat broader as it includes a competitiveness dimension in a similar manner to the performance pyramid of McNair et al.

Figure 6.4: The results and determinants framework

	Dimensions of performance	Types of measures
Results	Competitiveness	Relative market share and position Sales growth Measures of the customer base
	Financial	Profitability Liquidity Capital structure Market ratios
Determinants	Service quality	Reliability Responsiveness Aesthetics/appearance Cleanliness/tidiness Comfort Friendliness Communication Courtesy Competence Access Availability Security
	Flexibility	Volume flexibility Delivery speed flexibility Specification flexibility
	Resource utilisation	Productivity Efficiency
	Innovation	Performance of the innovation process Performance of individual innovations

(*Source:* Brignall et al., 1991, p.35)

Fitzgerald and Moon (1996) argue that it is essential to devise non-financial performance measures which capture the quality, service and flexibility issues that are paramount in customer-oriented service and product markets. By using the terms 'dimensions of performance' and 'types of measures', Brignall et al. link the strategic issues and their measurement in a similar manner to Kaplan and Norton through their 'goals' and 'measures'. The models are very similar and reflect the requirement for performance measurement to be much broader than the traditional financial ones.

It is important to recognise that each business organisation will have to develop its own measures of performance. These will be a product of the type of business, its competitive strategy, its technological background, its organisational structure and so on. Regardless of specific design, each framework will have to ensure that performance measures are derived from the corporate strategy, include external and internal measures, include non-financial as well as financial measures and make explicit the trade-offs between various measures of performance.

Designing balanced scorecard measures

While the Kaplan and Norton framework has four elements and the Brignall et al. has six, any organisation designing such a framework will include as many elements as is considered appropriate: for example, the General Electric Company in the USA measured performance across eight dimensions. The design of any such framework must have the following objectives:

- to identify the measure that best communicates the meaning of strategy;
- to align individual, organisational and cross-departmental initiatives;
- to identify entirely new processes for meeting customer and shareholder objectives.

The approach is to:

- list objectives for each perspective;
- describe measures for each objective;
- illustrate how each measure can be quantified;
- formulate a heuristic as to how the measures are linked.

Advantages and problems of the balanced scorecard approach

The general concept of using a more sophisticated measuring system for performance, balancing a range of factors, internal and external, long and short term, is clearly sensible and if successfully achieved would meet the normal criticisms of the profit measure. The old adage 'you get what you measure' means managers will respond to the measuring system and attempt to meet published targets; if there are costs and trade-offs involved these will be on dimensions that are not measured and published. This issue was considered in Chapter 3 which heralded the move to a more balanced approach.

There may be a problem with the volume of information. It can be argued that the balanced scorecard reflects how managers actually work, that they look at a profit report and mentally impose that information on a variety of other factors (a mental balanced scorecard). But receiving new information on all these factors is an increased load, and there are limits to everyone's information processing capacity, even if these limits are difficult to ascertain. The balanced scorecard can provide those at the top of a diversified organisation with an excessive load. However, it could be argued that the load is no more excessive than the present voluminous monthly report packages that are familiar in most organisations. A structured summary using the balanced scorecard could be more effective than senior managers merely looking at the operating statement page of the report and ignoring all the supplementary detail. The balance between attributes may be difficult to make but at least the information is present.

There is a further problem in whether the balanced scorecard implies more detailed central control. Is it merely a top-management 'command and control' technique, where targets are made more detailed which ensures that managers carry out tasks in a particular manner? This may be appropriate in a multibranch environment where identical standards may be desirable, but not necessarily where a manager has the normal autonomy of a divisional manager.

Increased central control may be essential with the globalisation of business. Multinationals cannot easily look at businesses in different countries as entirely separate, with the flexibility to work to disparate standards and to promote and exploit a global brand in a range of ways. However, if a divisional manager can validly be measured on simple measures such as profit, cash flow and the achievement of budget, without any distortion of strategic policy, the central information load can be considerably reduced, and delegation of authority can be far more effective.

Practical experience of a balanced approach to performance measurement

In 1952, the General Electric Company (USA) proposed eight measures of organisational performance (see Anthony et al., 1984):

- profitability measured by residual income;
- market position – market share;
- productivity – of capital as well as labour; comparisons being made with competitors as well as internal trends over time;
- product leadership – development of existing and new products;
- personnel development – recruitment and training of skilled personnel and managers for the present and future needs of the company;
- employee attitudes – motivation;
- public responsibility – ethics, community responsibility, pollution, safety, information disclosure;
- balance of long-range and short-range goals – do methods of achieving short-term profit weaken future prospects?

A formal system of this sort was unusual, though most companies look at a wide range of measures at different times. Normally, most company systems deal with the issues separately rather than as an integrated package. The above approach, while predating the more conscious balanced views, contains features of the strategic planning process which itself includes aspects of marketing, internal process, product development and financial areas.

Brander Brown and McDonnell (1995) conducted a pilot study to develop a balanced scorecard for use by large hotel companies. The study was in three stages. The first stage was to identify the hotel's visions and corresponding objectives; the second, to determine the hotel's critical success factors in relation to those objectives; and the third, to develop an appropriate balance of performance measures to support the critical success factors.

Having developed a balanced scorecard for a hotel, the following implications were considered important. Initially, there appears to be a need to define the business unit for which the scorecard is being developed, as this would differ with organisation level. There was a clear need for the balanced scorecard components to be reviewed and updated on a regular basis. This was considered essential to reflect the dynamic and turbulent nature of the hotel industry so that different attributes could be prioritised to reflect the changing environment (in a similar manner to accounting information systems for contingent variables, which will be considered in Chapter 8). Finally, the developed scorecard could accommodate other aspects of hotel activities that were not currently made explicit in traditional performance measurement systems.

Newing (1995) reported the use of the balanced scorecard approach within National Westminster Life Assurance, where it was found that the approach 'helps manage conflicting priorities in a manner which recognises trade-offs which may occur between different business perspectives'. The scorecard had also been used to communicate and delegate business priorities for staff understanding and as a basis for reward. Evans et al. (1996) reported that Abbey National Finance and Investment Services had adopted the balanced scorecard approach. A developed scorecard for an international insurance broker is reproduced in Figure 6.5, which gives the four dimensions of the balanced view without the key success factors or measures which are required to monitor the performance outcomes. The Abbey National approach sees the balanced scorecard within a framework where the management information system, strategic management and the balanced scorecard are seen as interacting and supporting processes which provide a programme of change as driven by the mission statement and interpreted through the critical success factors embodied in that framework.

Dinesh and Palmer (1998) argue that the balanced scorecard approach is based on the same philosophies as management by objectives which employ the use of critical success factors. Both are management systems based on goal congruence as a means of improving organisational performance. This assertion may lead to a debate about the manner in which organisational goals are developed, aggregated and employed within a management by objective process. However, Dinesh and Palmer are more concerned with the failure of management by objectives programmes and how the weaknesses in these programmes may impact on the balanced scorecard method, as the two systems are so similar. They argue that management by objectives systems have not been completely successful because of their partial implementation. The time and energy needed to instigate, develop and maintain such processes are quite considerable and may not be cost-effective. They also argue that the balanced scorecard approach has its origins in the human relations school of management, which may be easier to develop for smaller operational groups than whole organisations wishing to move forward on a series of strategic developments. Hence, Dinesh and Palmer believe that the balanced scorecard may not, in the longer term, be maintained.

Figure 6.5: Balanced scorecard example of an international insurance broker

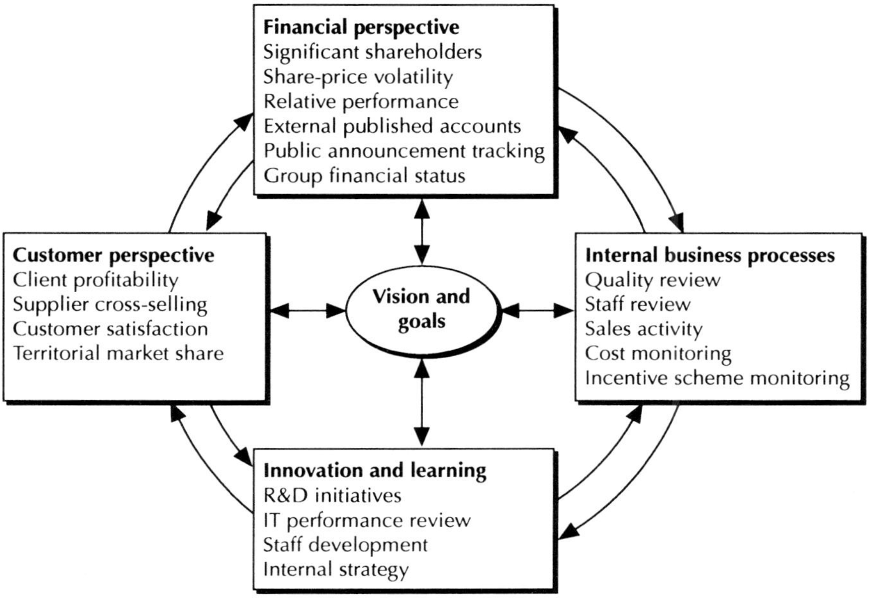

Financial perspective
Significant shareholders
Share-price volatility
Relative performance
External published accounts
Public announcement tracking
Group financial status
Customer perspective
Client profitability
Supplier cross-selling
Customer satisfaction
Territorial market share
Vision and goals
Internal business processes
Quality review
Staff review
Sales activity
Cost monitoring
Incentive scheme monitoring
Innovation and learning
R&D initiatives
IT performance review
Staff development
Internal strategy

(*Source:* Evans et al., 1996, p.23)

Murphy (1998) argued that the balanced scorecard approach could be linked to the multiple constituency view of organisational objectives. When applied to the National Health Service (NHS) he considered the four major stakeholders to be the patients, the general public, the Treasury, and the professionals working within the NHS. He argued that each constituent group has an interest in equity, efficiency and responsiveness, but that each will define success in different ways and thus provide different assessments of performance. If the objectives, definitions of success and performance indicators can be solicited for each constituency then a balanced scorecard of the NHS may be established. This 'balanced picture' may, Murphy argues, have the profile shown in Figure 6.6.

Figure 6.6: NHS balanced scorecard framework

Efficiency
Patient expectations
Effectiveness
Evaluation

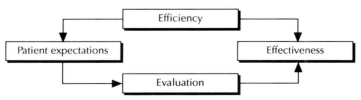

(*Source:* Murphy, 1998)

This generic framework can then be developed by using specific performance indicators for particular selections of the NHS. Murphy (1998) puts forward one for cardiovascular operations. The NHS scorecard is different in nature to the profit-focused private sector ones as effectiveness is seen as the outcome (to replace the financial perspective) while efficiency, patients' expectations and evolution are seen as the necessary determinants of that effectiveness.

Summary

The general development of balanced scorecards does provide an integrated performance model which is needed to draw back from the unidimensional financial aspects of performance as demonstrated in Chapter 3 and established to be dysfunctional.

The balanced scorecard approach helps move the performance debate away from the short term issues of financial reporting to the longer term strategic and competitive issues while still recognising short term performance measures. In particular the Kaplan and Norton (1992) framework sees financial performance as an outcome from the other perspectives of customer, internal business and innovation and learning. The results–determinant framework of Brignall et al. (1991) has a very similar stance but includes competitiveness as a result rather than a determinant of financial performance. Regardless of origin and history, the balanced approach to performance measurement is a rational step forward to redress the problems of pure financial measurement while including the longer term more strategic focus.

7 Relating Performance Measurement and Strategy

Introduction

This chapter seeks to consider the strategic issues that are bound up in an organisation's performance measurement and organisational frameworks. Chandler (1962) argued that a strategy of product diversification has caused many organisations to divisionalise their structure. In more recent decades the movement has been for large organisations to move to a framework which includes strategic business units (SBUs) rather than divisions, so providing more scope for management flexibility.

This chapter returns to the theme of internal business processes (see Figure 7.1) by considering organisational structures and the relevant performance measurement issues for particular business strategies. It outlines various models that may be relevant to further the effectiveness of an organisation.

Figure 7.1: A framework for studying corporate performance measurement

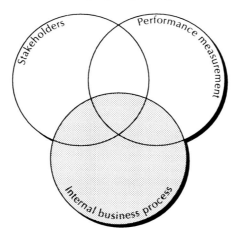

The Scott (1971) matrix portrayed the development of a business in four stages, which linked to different organisational structures and their particular attributes. The Scott matrix views the development of organisational structures through growth in size and complexity. Initial growth in size is seen as leading to the development of decentralised, functionally based organisations. With increasing complexity, the structure becomes more product-based and quasi-autonomous, with strategy held centrally – the classic multidivisional company.

The final stage suggests that, as organisations become so diverse, the holding of a central strategy is replaced by the delegation of individual strategies to divisions or strategic business units. The Scott matrix presents a logical progression of growth and complexity leading to different structures, but any large, diverse company may adopt different control mechanisms and performance measures for different parts of the business at any one time – so control and performance measurement of core business may be different from peripheral business units.

Figure 7.2: Four stages of organisational development

	Owner-manager	Growth in size	Growth in complexity but central strategy	Highly diverse, no central, strategy: set by business units
Stage	I	II	III	IV
Product line	Single	Single	Multiple	Multiple
Distribution	Single	Single	Multiple	Multiple
Organisational structure	Little or no formal structure	Functionally based and integrated	Product market based and quasi-autonomous	Product market based and largely autonomous

(*Adapted from:* Scott, 1971)

This chapter presents the case for the development of the divisional (M-form) organisation and considers performance measures that may be applicable to it with their resultant problems. The chapter then considers the strategic business unit before different performance measures are viewed as being appropriate or otherwise to particular business strategies.

Multidivisional organisations

Emmanuel et al. (1990) argue that the major advantage of decentralised and multinational organisations in particular is that it allows different levels of management to 'concentrate on those issues with which they are best placed to deal'. The M-form organisation, which operates as a series of investment centres, should provide for effective performance and profit maximisation (Williamson, 1975) through the following three attributes:

1. The efficient allocation of resources within the organisation. If an organisation is compared with a capital market then headquarters could be considered to be making investments, by allocating resources, in different divisions. External funds raised by headquarters will have a lower cost than any individual division could obtain. The funds are then allocated on a competitive basis between divisions, and the efficiency of these funds measured through the use of performance indicators.

2. The allocation of day-to-day operational decision-making to largely autonomous divisions ensures that corporate communication channels are not

overloaded with detailed operational data which has been filtered out on lower levels. This frees corporate communication channels for the dissemination of strategy downwards, and the flow of summarised information (including performance measures) upwards to headquarters.

3. M-form structures should minimise suboptimal behaviour. The separation of strategic decisions and day-to-day operating decisions to headquarters and divisions respectively reduces the complexity of decision-making. It also reduces risk, as each level understands its environment and operations more fully.

Theory would suggest that hierarchies, such as divisional companies, and integrated organisations are only beneficial over markets if it is more economical to organise transactions through those hierarchies. Hence, any managerial costs must be less than the transaction costs of operating through the markets. The delegation of decision-making to divisional managers will automatically increase managerial costs through the increased monitoring of performance in order to ensure that delegated authority is not being misused. It is possible for the performance of one division to be enhanced at the expense of the total organisation, which may be a product of separation of activities and over-competitive behaviour among divisions. Emmanuel et al. (1990) stated that the loss of central control results in a higher incidence of non-programmed decisions for divisional managers. It is essential that these are taken using a full organisational rather than merely a single division framework of objectives.

Williamson (1970, 1975) puts forward procedures for the implementation of divisional structure as follows:

- Identification of divisional boundaries;
- Assignment of quasi-autonomous status for each division, so determining the extent of divisional autonomy;
- Allocation of company resources to divisions;
- Use of performance measures and reward schemes to monitor divisional activities;
- The performance of strategic planning whenever possible.

It is the performance measurement issues that are particularly relevant to this chapter. Ezzamel and Hart (1987) consider that the monitoring of divisional organisations can operate at three different levels: advanced, contemporaneous (current) and ex-post. The advanced level involves reviews of divisional proposed courses of action, which may include capital investment appraisal approval by headquarters. Current evaluation entails continuous monitoring of divisional performance through a series of measurement mechanisms and targets, while the ex-post evaluation involves end-of-period performance evaluation.

Traditional accounting methods of divisional performance

Measures of divisional performance have been traditionally profit based. There is substantial research over a long period demonstrating the continued use of profit performance measures and either return on investment (ROI) or return on capital employed (ROCE) as the main measures of divisional performance (Tomkins, 1973; Reece and Cool, 1978; Vancil, 1979). Solomons (1965) gave three reasons why some sort of performance index based on profitability would be useful:

1. As a guide to central management in assessing the efficiency of each division as an economic entity.
2. As an end to central management in assessing the efficiency with which divisional managers discharge their duties.
3. To guide divisional managers in making decisions in respect of the daily activities of their own divisions.

A major problem with this approach is to devise performance measures which do not encourage divisional managers to pursue policies that are beneficial to their own divisions but detrimental to the organisation as a whole. Drury (1985) summarised the work of Shillington (1982) in the following three rules:

1. Divisional profit should not be increased by any action which reduces total organisational profit.
2. Each division's profit should be as independent as possible of performance efficiency and managerial decisions elsewhere in the company.
3. Each division's profit should reflect items which are subject to any substantial degree of control by divisional management or their subordinates.

The traditional measures of profit, ROI and ROCE, have all been seen to have problems in application, interpretation and resultant impacts. Residual income (RI), while having fewer problems, as it employs an opportunity cost of capital in a similar manner to internal rate of return (IRR) and net present value (NPV), may drive short-termism in particular circumstances. Chapter 4 spent considerable time considering the development and application of economic value analysis which uses and integrates the concepts of RI, IRR and NPV. Because the problems of financial measures have already been expressed in previous chapters and will continue to be so in later chapters, this section will not rehearse the arguments again. Instead, it will merely act as a reminder of the problems with financially-based performance measures, which include:

▪ concentration on the short term to the detriment of longer-term performance;
▪ financial corporate objectives may neglect other equally valued corporate objectives;
▪ manipulation of the figures;
▪ interdependency of the divisions mean that any manager may pursue policies that are dysfunctional to the whole;
▪ divisional profit measure must be dependent on other divisions;

- the level of risk associated with each division may be ignored by headquarters, which is seeking a weighted average return attributable to the main stakeholders.

Developments in the organisational structures of large companies are resulting in the fourth stage of the Scott matrix to be realised (Figure 7.2). This stage reflects a position where companies are highly diverse, operating in multiple-product markets, and where strategy is largely set by business units rather than being delegated from headquarters. This type of organisation requires a new look at performance measurement that is less financially based and more strategically focused.

A new agenda

As developed earlier in this chapter, Williamson (1970, 1975) based his work on the premise that headquarters developed, set and delegated strategic decisions, and that divisional managers pursued operational initiatives to meet delegated performance measures encapsulating that strategy. Many divisions are now responsible for their own strategies, so that different divisions may be pursuing different strategies and consequently require a different set of performance measurement criteria. Hall (1978) described how General Electric introduced the idea of strategic business units (SBUs). He outlined that an SBU was based on the following principles:

- the divisionalised firm should be managed as a 'portfolio' of businesses, with each business unit serving a clearly defined product-market segment with a clearly defined strategy;
- each business unit in the portfolio should develop a strategy tailored to its capabilities and competitive needs, but consistent with the overall capabilities and needs.

Hall went further and identified four steps which required to be operationalised for the concept of SBUs to be realised:

1. identification of strategic business units;
2. strategic analysis of these units to ascertain their competitive position and long-term product-market attractiveness;
3. strategic management of these units, given their overall positioning;
4. strategic follow-up and reappraisal of SBUs and corporate performance.

Once these steps have been recognised, Broadbent and Cullen (1995) argue that the performance measurement and appraisal systems applicable to SBUs are those applicable to any strategically minded organisation. Rather than present an exhaustive literature on the variation of performance measures for different strategic frameworks, this section will develop three major themes. They are those put forward using a product portfolio matrix, management-style framework and the development of the Porter (1985) generic chain.

Product portfolio matrix

Hall (1978) emphasised the need for different performance measurement and appraisal systems for business units holding different positions in the product portfolio matrix. Such a classification system is that of dogs, problem child, stars and cash cows (Figure 7.3).

Figure 7.3: Product portfolio matrix

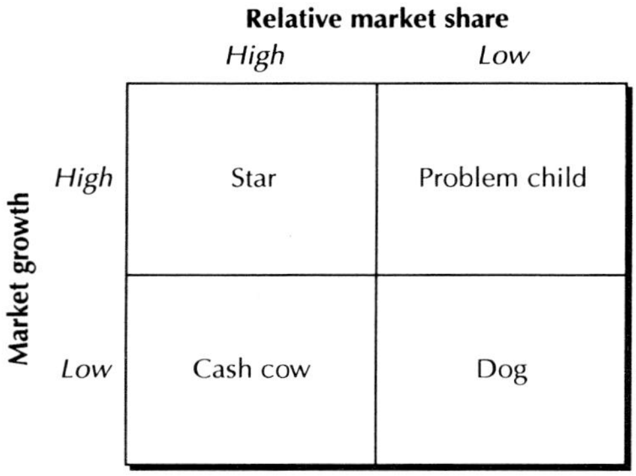

| | | Relative market share | |
		High	Low
Market growth	High	Star	Problem child
	Low	Cash cow	Dog

The product portfolio matrix developed by the Boston Consultancy Group classifies product and businesses by market share and market growth. In this, a cash cow refers to a product or business with high market share and low market growth, a dog refers to one with low market share and low growth, a problem child has a low market share and high growth, and a star has high growth and high market share. In the CIMA *Official Terminology* (1991) a cash-flow interpretation is superimposed on the matrix, and this is reproduced in Figure 7.4.

Figure 7.4: Product portfolio matrix and cash flow

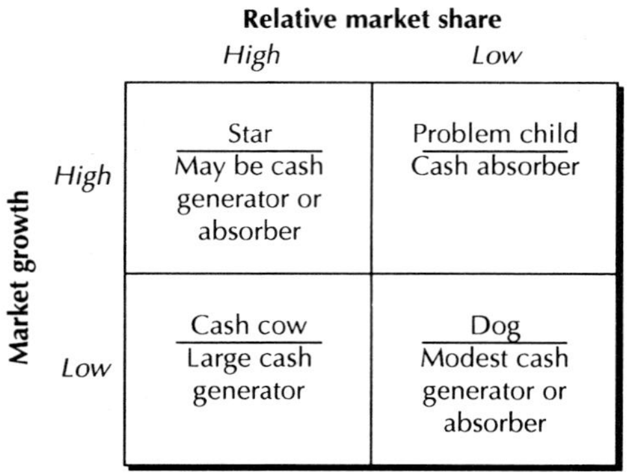

| | | Relative market share | |
		High	Low
Market growth	High	Star May be cash generator or absorber	Problem child Cash absorber
	Low	Cash cow Large cash generator	Dog Modest cash generator or absorber

(Adapted from: CIMA, 1991)

Hall (1978) argues that different performance measures would be relevant for different quadrants of the matrix. While CIMA has adopted a cash-flow focus, a more strategic focus can be considered. It would be foolish to inflict a series of profit- and cash-focused performance measures on either a problem child or a star. These two quadrants would be better assessed by using measures which reflect the growth in customers relative to competitors, and how successful market penetration has been to date. It would be appropriate to ensure that cash cows and dogs are generating profits and cash flows; measures of ROI and ROCE would be particularly appropriate as the short-term focus of these measures may be used to ensure that further investment is modest and profitability is maximised. The same arguments can be considered in the phases of a product life cycle (Figure 7.5).

Figure 7.5: Product life cycle

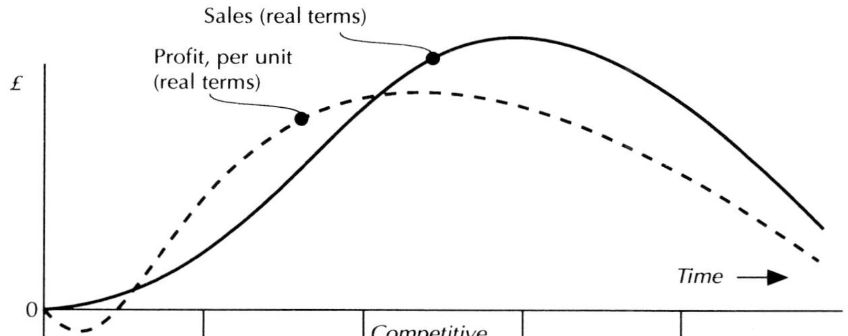

Stage	Introduction	Growth	Competitive turbulence	Maturity	Decline
Sales	Low	Rising rapidly	Slowing	Peak sales	Declining
Prices	High	Falling	Low	Low	Falling
Profit/unit	Negative	High rising	Declining	Average	Declining
Customers	Innovators	Early adopters	Early majority	Late majority	Laggards
Competitors	Few	Growing number	Shakeout begins	Declining numbers	Further decline
Overall strategy	Create awareness R&D critical	Market-share penetration	Protect and strengthen niche	Protect share – manage for earnings. Emphasise competitive costs	Reduce expenditures and harvest

(*Source:* Wilson, 1991, p.88)

The product life cycle concept maps the development and decline of a product by sales history. Different stages of the cycle will require different performance measures that are market based up to maturity and then profit and cash-flow focused in maturity and decline.

It would be illogical to go through the process of strategic analysis and then to continue to measure performance by annual profit targets. In 1978 Hall reported:

Most firms have gone only halfway with the SBU concept – they position the product-market segments and then go right on rewarding and promoting managers on traditional criteria. In the end, the companies which make the SBU concept work will be those which change all management systems: developing and rewarding SBU managers differently depending on their SBU position and the strategic handling which is appropriate for their element of the portfolio.

Since 1978 there have been significant developments in the way performance measures are derived and measured. There has been a shift towards more strategic thinking and the notion of critical success factor analysis. In addition, the Kaplan and Norton (1992) and Fitzgerald et al. (1991) frameworks which were presented in Chapter 6 have been seen to reflect a more balanced, strategically driven performance measurement approach.

Strategy and performance measures

A major study of SBUs was made adopting the framework developed by Miles and Snow (1978) in which they classify organisational type by strategic process. The basis of the study by Hall (1978) was to research the link between organisational type and their control procedures, which included performance measures. The Miles and Snow (1978) matrix is presented in Figure 7.6.

Figure 7.6: Organisational classifications

Organis'n type	Characteristics of strategic decision-making		
	Dominant objectives	Preferred strategies	Planning and control
Defender	Desire for a secure and stable niche in market	Specialisation; cost-efficient production; marketing emphasises price and service to defend current business; tendency to vertical integration	Centralised, detailed control; emphasis on cost-efficiency; extensive use of formal planning
Prospector	Location and exploitation of new product and market opportunities	Growth through product and market development (often in spurts); constant monitoring of environmental change; multiple technologies	Emphasis on flexibility, decentralised control, use of *ad hoc* measurements
Analyser	Desire to match new ventures to present shape of business	Steady growth through market penetration; exploitation of applied research; followers in the market	Very complicated; co-ordinating roles between functions (e.g. product managers); intensive planning

(*Source:* Miles and Snow, 1978)

The three organisational types put forward by Miles and Snow each has different objectives. A defender wishes to maintain current niche markets, a prospector seeks to go out and establish new product-market opportunities, while an analyser wishes to grow into new markets which fit into current activities.

Simons (1987) investigated the relationship between business strategy and accounting-based control systems in 76 SBUs. He used the Miles and Snow typology presented in Figure 7.6 to identify different organisational types. The study concluded that firms following different strategies do indeed employ different accounting control systems. He found that successful prospector firms seem to attach a great deal of importance to the use of forecast data, set tight performance measures but do not use tight cost control measures, and monitor outputs carefully. These accounting measures balance the other measures inherent in the prospector with its emphasis on flexibility, decentralised control and *ad hoc* measurement systems. Defenders, particularly large firms, appear to use their control processes less intensively; in fact, negative correlations were noted between profit performance and tight budget goals and intensive performance monitoring.

Govindarajan and Gupta (1985) studied the linkages between strategy and incentive bonus systems and the effectiveness of strategic business units. They used a different matrix from that of Miles and Snow to classify the strategic positioning of companies. They used the generic terms 'build' and 'harvest' which represent the extremes of a continuum. The 'build' represents a mission to increase market share, while 'harvest' represents the maximisation of short-term earnings and cash flow. The results of the study can be summarised by saying that, in build SBU companies, the performance measures that were used to establish general manager bonus levels were based on long-run criteria and subjective, so allowing for the strategic building process. The long-run criteria were measures of product development, market development, personnel development and political/public affairs involvement, all of which one would associate with strategically oriented SBUs and 'holding' companies alike.

Goold and Campbell (1987) looked at the different philosophies for managing diversity within leading British firms. The introduction to their article states,

> Many large companies today operate in a range of different businesses. These companies need to fine-tune their management styles to the specific requirements of each business in their portfolio. But they also wish to avoid unmanageable organisational complexity and, as far as possible, to operate with a single, consistent, widely understood corporate culture throughout the company. Managing diversity therefore causes particular problems and conflicts.

The study identified three main different central management 'styles': strategic planning, strategic control and financial control. Each will be considered.

Corporate management in strategic planning companies believe that the centre should participate in and influence the development of business unit strategies. Their influence takes two forms: establishing a planning process and contributing to strategic thinking. In general, they place rather less emphasis on financial controls. Performance targets are set flexibly, and are reviewed within the context of long-term progress.

The centre of strategic control companies is concerned with the plans of its business units, but it believes in autonomy for business unit managers. Plans are reviewed in a formal planning process. The objective is to upgrade the quality of the thinking. But the centre does not want to advocate strategies or interfere with the major decisions. Control is maintained by the use of financial targets and strategic objectives. These are agreed with the centre, and business unit managers are expected to meet the standards.

Financial control companies focus on annual profit targets. There are no long-term planning systems and no strategy documents. The centre limits its role to approving investments and budgets, and monitoring performance. Targets are expected to be stretching, and once they are agreed they become part of a contract between the business unit and the centre. Failure to deliver the promised figures can lead to management changes.

The study also identified three main philosophies for building and managing a diverse portfolio. These styles broadly correspond to the three most popular strategic management styles and are described above.

The philosophy of operating a series of core businesses where the company commits itself to a few industries and sets out to achieve considerable market share in these industries is best managed by using the strategic planning style.

The financial control style of management is best suited to the management of businesses that are either classified to be at the mature parts of their product cycles or within the cash cow and dog quadrants of the strategic matrix. These businesses may exhibit extensive diversity across industries, but each is at the same maturity level of its development. The financial control style employing short-term financial performance measures would be appropriate for such companies. It may also be the case that such companies may be the subject of partial disposal, as productive assets are not replaced, so releasing other assets for disposal.

Diverse, growing businesses are best managed by using a strategic control style of management. Their emphasis is on diversity rather than focused operations, so that a portfolio is established that spreads risk across industries and geographic areas.

From our point of view, an interesting finding coming from the study was that companies tend to employ a uniform style across most of their businesses, and that changes in style seldom occur. The authors suggest that this reflects the importance of simplicity and consistency in organisational structures and systems. Mismatch is avoided by ensuring a close match between the nature of the businesses in the portfolio and the strategic management style. Three detailed case studies found that both strategic planning and strategic control companies awarded senior staff bonuses by using subjective performance measures based around strategic fulfilment. The financial control company used actual profit compared with budget profit for bonus calculations. The latter company did, however, operate in mature markets with cash cow or dog types of business; hence the performance measures for bonus awards may be considered wholly appropriate.

Returning to the Miles and Snow (1978) characteristics of strategic decision-making matrix put forward in Figure 7.6, a series of performance measures may be derived from the critical success factors. Such a matrix is presented in Table 7.1.

Table 7.1: Performance measures appropriate for different organisational types

Organisational type	Performance measures
Defender	Cost-efficiency of production methods
	Customer satisfaction
	Maintenance of relative market share
Prospector	New product from research
	Speed to market for new products
	Development of new technologies
	Flexibility of manufacturing capability
	Growth of market share
Analyser	Development of market share
	Product development

If the particular performance measures for each organisational type are set within the balanced scorecard (see Figure 6.5) then the balance between the different perspectives will vary. For example, the innovation and learning perspective would have greater emphasis for a prospector than an analyser, which in turn would be stronger than a defender.

Another view of strategic performance attributes may be derived using the Porter (1985) model of the generic value chain, which is a detailed organisational analysis within the Porter (1985) value system (see Figure 4.4). The value chain for an organisation is presented in Figure 7.7.

Figure 7.7: The value chain

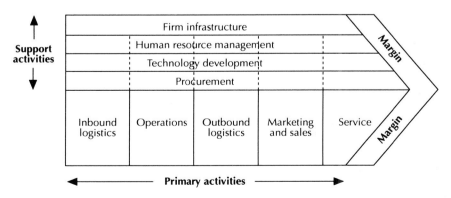

(*Source:* Porter, 1985, reproduced in Johnson and Scholes, 1997)

Porter argues than an understanding of the strategic capability of any organisation must commence by identifying the value activities within itself. The model recognises five primary activities and four linked support activities. They are summarised below:

1. *Inbound logistics:* receiving, storing and distributing input to the product or service.
2. *Operations:* transforming various inputs into final products or services.
3. *Outbound logistics:* collect, store and delivery of products to the customers.
4. *Marketing and sales:* means whereby customers are aware of the product or service and hence the desire to purchase.
5. *Service:* the services which enhance or maintain value of the product or service to the customer.

Each of the primary activities is linked to support activities which include procurement, technological development, human resource management and general company infrastructure services. Porter (1985) goes further than just providing a model of the value activities; he also provides a series of competencies that are capable of measurement for each of the primary and supporting activities. Such a series of competencies are presented in Figure 7.8, where the functional names are used for the primary and support activities. The figure provides a series of competences or critical success factors for each activity which could be converted into measures of performance.

A combined value system and value chain is presented for a can-maker and canner in Figure 7.9. The two companies are part of the value system for the industry and provide support for one another. The figure illustrates the key support competences of the can-maker that would require measurement to maintain and enhance the link with the canner. The links between can-maker and canner demonstrated in Figure 7.9 may not be obvious at first, but they represent key linkages between the two companies' joint operations within the value chain. They include the following:

1. Can design for specific segments of the canner product range.
2. Speed of can filling for the canner.
3. Stock management systems which could include JIT.
4. Sales and purchases should be linked to avoid overstocking for both can-maker and canner.
5. Support for the canner to ensure smooth canning operations.

Particular performance measures could be designed to meet these particular linkages.

Figure 7.8: Sources of differentiation

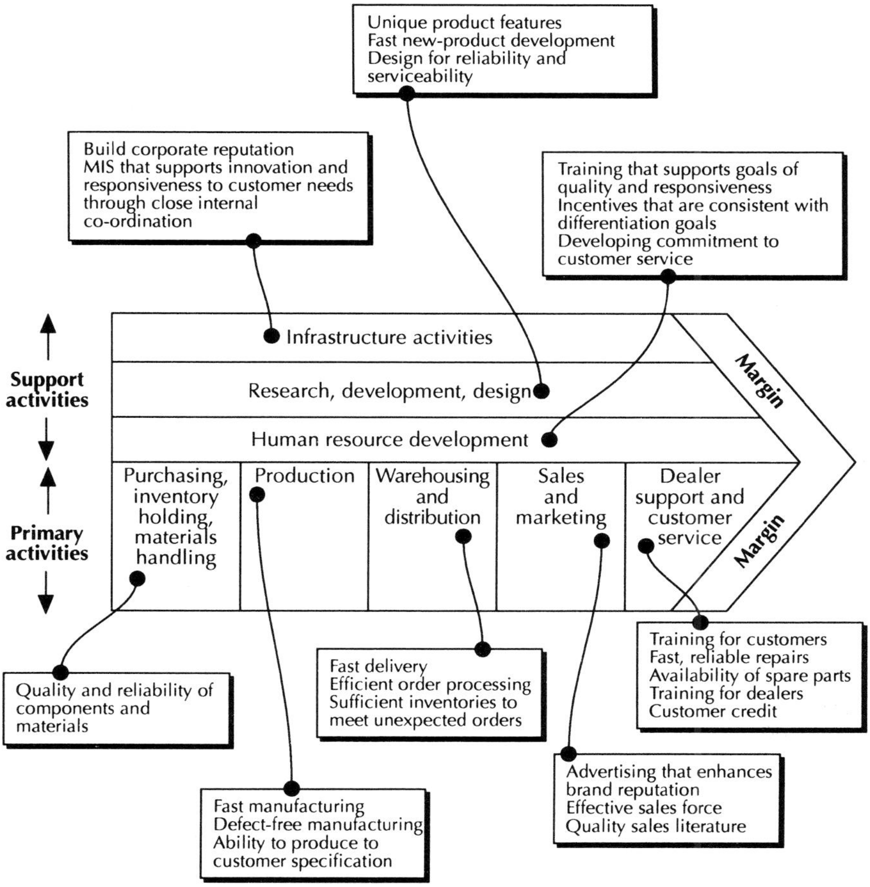

Unique product features
Fast new-product development
Design for reliability and
serviceability

Build corporate reputation
MIS that supports innovation and
responsiveness to customer needs
through close internal
co-ordination

Training that supports goals of
quality and responsiveness
Incentives that are consistent with
differentiation goals
Developing commitment to
customer service

**Support
activities**

Infrastructure activities

Research, development, design

Human resource development

Margin

**Primary
activities**

Purchasing, inventory holding, materials handling	Production	Warehousing and distribution	Sales and marketing	Dealer support and customer service

Margin

Quality and reliability of
components and
materials

Fast delivery
Efficient order processing
Sufficient inventories to
meet unexpected orders

Training for customers
Fast, reliable repairs
Availability of spare parts
Training for dealers
Customer credit

Fast manufacturing
Defect-free manufacturing
Ability to produce to
customer specification

Advertising that enhances
brand reputation
Effective sales force
Quality sales literature

(*Source:* Porter, 1985, p.216)

Figure 7.9: Value chain for canned goods

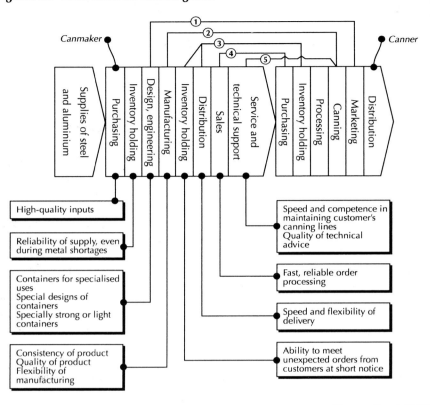

(Source: Grant, 1995)

Summary

This chapter has linked the requirement to amend and adapt performance measures for different stages in the business's growth which are reflected in different organisation structures. It has also demonstrated the need to amend the performance-measurement process for different stages within the product life cycle and for different strategic positionings of divisions and strategic business units. Performance measures will need to be amended as the strategic position of the company changes, in addition to its particular product life cycles. Each will be a product of its environment, which forms part of the focus of Chapter 8.

8 A Contingency Theory for Measurement?

Introduction

The essential theme of this short book has been the changing nature of business processes, management cultures and their related control issues. Performance matrices have had to adapt in order to monitor this constantly required adaptation by organisations. The emphasis has moved from product and service generation to the satisfaction of customers by providing quality goods and services at acceptable price levels. We have considered various techniques that may move towards this end, but basic questions still remain. Are performance-measurement indexes and their supporting information systems sufficiently flexible and informative to provide not only adequate but developmental management information? Before we attempt to answer this question it would be useful to consider the general contingency theory approach to management accounting prior to examining specific studies that reflect current and future organisational changes.

Figure 8.1: A framework for studying corporate performance measurement

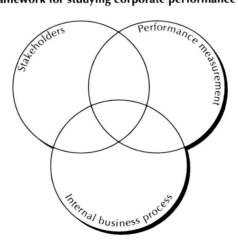

For this particular chapter the framework for studying corporate performance measurement (Figure 8.1) does not have any of its elements shaded. Each previous chapter has used this mechanism to emphasise the focus of the narrative, but this chapter is different. It attempts to provide an integrative approach that sees the three elements constantly relating to one another and hence changing their narrative in a unique manner for any particular organisation. The framework adopted is that of contingency theory, which is more reflective than the other models we have considered so far. In being reflective it provides a heuristic for understanding processes rather than techniques for implementation, and may provide a rationale to explain current corporate performance measures adopted in your organisation.

An outline of contingency theory

In simple terms, contingency theory is based on the following assumptions and principles:

- organisations are influenced by their environment and their history: by such factors as the technology employed, the size of the firm, the competitiveness of the market, the stability of the environment, the people involved and the ownership of the firm;
- hence each organisation is unique;
- structure, control and performance-measurement systems in each firm will be influenced by the environment of the firm, and will be different from one firm to another;
- there is no one best system for all firms.

With these principles in mind it is important *not* to make certain deductions from these basic statements.

In large organisations, it is not appropriate to assume that all parts of the organisation are affected in the same way by contingent factors. It may well be appropriate to look at the separate component organisations and their environmental settings. In the same manner, it is not appropriate to assume that all organisations in the same environment will respond in the same way to develop similar structures, control and performance systems. People make different judgements, so creating disparate structures and systems, as there can be apparently small but critical differences between firms in an industry, which make some more successful than others, facilitating a large range of solutions. A successful firm can fund advanced manufacturing technology ahead of its rivals, and can then make more progress using TQM, JIT, benchmarking, etc., to enhance its operations. A less successful firm may require business process re-engineering projects.

It should be noted that there are pressures other than contingent factors towards uniform systems, the current example being the emphasis on good corporate governance and the need for listed companies to report on internal control. This means that most non-executive directors regard internal audit as essential. The same belief in conventional best practice ensures that most firms insist on the use of large audit firms, monthly accounts, the use of NPV in investment justification and so on. Another factor which works towards identical systems, often employed by smaller firms, is the development of commercially available software for specific industries, examples of which include systems for motor dealers, doctors, hotels, theatres and the like.

Simply stated, contingency theory is intuitively appealing. It seems sensible, as it provides general explanations of visible differences between organisations. Advocates of a contingency framework have claimed at various times the following advantages:

- It provides a statement of formal links in testable form between the key factors of the environment, the organisation, the management system, the accounting information system and hence performance measurement.
- It links management accounting to other management and social sciences theories. Benefit is gained from common approaches to management and organisational problems, in that research findings in one field would be evidence in another field to the extent that they supported the theory.
- It explains behavioural studies of budgeting and organisational behaviour by trying to fit into a consistent framework. The ideal is to establish some form of comparability between behavioural studies as a step towards being able to synthesise the lessons to be learnt.

Features that are common to most studies of contingency theory provide an emphasis on change in organisations and the environment, reflecting an awareness of environmental complexity which cannot be modelled with a few simple variables. Organisations' adaptive responses can differ, even when the environmental factors appear to be the same. There is a clear attempt to identify and study the impact of key environmental factors. While the earlier studies stressed much the same factors as Burns and Stalker (1961) and Woodward (1965) (size, technology, product variety, task complexity), later studies tended to highlight factors such as environmental uncertainty. The studies showed concern with overall organisation structure as well as particular aspects of management such as management accounting, which recognised that structure is itself a control device.

While much of the work around and involving contingency theory approaches attempts to map relationships between variables and management processes, it provides little in perspective knowledge or technique-based solutions for managers. It does, however, signal to management the need to give consideration to a broader range of issues and stakeholders than the internal management processes would normally assume. Taken in the context of a survival model of the firm then every organisation must be ready and able to respond to the changing environment. An inability to do so would result in decline and eventual failure. Hence, contingency theory does not provide a basis for action but attempts to document the reflect postures adopted by management in the development of the organisation.

There have been several criticisms levelled at contingency theory, which include those of research method and the reliability of the results, but more importantly for us are the major criticisms put forward by Dent (1990). He takes the view that organisations can create their own environments. They are not merely responses to environmental uncertainties that are seeking to survive in a reactive manner. Organisational managers have the ability to redefine the environment, making the boundaries between the firm and its environment less clear-cut. Dent goes further by stating that 'new planning and control systems provide a means of re-orchestrating responsibilities and linkages to the environment, facilitating organisational change, not just in a passive way, but proactively' (p.20). This may require a change in culture that requires the decoupling of an organisation from one combination of notions, relationships, practices and so on to be recoupled to another, but different, combination of factors that reflect that cultural change.

The change of management practices and the adoption of differing techniques including TQM, benchmarking, ABC, BPR, JIT, stakeholder analysis, customer orientation and so forth have all contributed to the manner, and culture, of how a particular organisation now operates in response to its environment. This means that performance measurement can no longer be a narrow, inflexible and static process. To remain effective it must be capable of continual adaptive change, hence the move towards the broader, more determinant frameworks considered within the balanced approaches to performance measurement put forward in Chapter 6.

The next section of this chapter considers three themes drawn from specific contingency research, studies that could be considered relevant, with adaptation, to more modern management issues. The three themes are technology, organisational structure and the environment.

Technology

Woodward (1965) recognised that different types of production techniques, which he defined as unit production, small-batch, large-batch and process production, influenced the design of internal accounting information systems and the manner of cost accumulation for performance measurement. The smaller the batch size the less there is need to use average figures and cost apportionment techniques. With process production the whole emphasis is on the average unit or average equivalent unit cost. Hence, technology has an impact on the accounting information system and resulting performance measures that are provided. In a more proactive manner, Piper (1978) demonstrated that task complexity is relevant in defining a financial control structure that should be provided for effective performance measurement. In a similar manner, Daft and MacIntosh (1978) identified task variety and knowledge as variables in management information system design.

Within modern manufacturing encompassing the JIT philosophy, the requirement may be to produce batches that vary from many to few depending on the requirements to meet, but not exceed, production requirements. If linked to ABC this provides an accounting system that can cope with dissimilar batch sizes and different products by emphasising cost driver measurement rather than volume attributes.

In a specific example Soin (1995) documents the introduction of an ABC system within the banking industry. Until the beginning of the 1980s cost control was not evident within the banking sector: there was no emphasis on cost or cost awareness. The banks operated within an oligopoly protected by prohibitively high entry barrier costs. Once the markets were deregulated then the banks needed to be acutely aware of their individual product costs. Because of the complexity and cross-subsidisation of the services offered by the banks it was particularly difficult to measure performance, trace and control costs for individual product offerings. Because of this complex product/process relationship and the high overhead cost base, ABC was considered to be particularly useful within a strategy that pursued increased profits to ensure adequate returns to shareholders. The aim of particular studies introducing ABC 'was to be able to identify the costs and services in the clearing department and to identify cost drivers of the activities in the value chain' (p.292). Its introduction was also an attempt to change the culture of the bank to that of a cost-aware and cost management organisation.

Organisational structure

Burns and Stalker (1961) argue there is a clear relationship between the organisational structure and the environment in which it operates. This theme will be developed to consider how the organisational structure, once established, affects the manner in which performance and control information is used.

Hopwood (1972) and Otley (1978) appeared to provide conflicting results about the relationship between structure and accounting information systems and their use. Hopwood, in a study of cost centres within an integrated steel plant, was able to recognise two different styles in the use of budgetary information. They were, firstly, budget-constrained, where the budget was the single most important factor in a superior's rigid evaluation of a subordinate. Secondly, a profit-conscious style, where long-run effectiveness was also considered in a more flexible manner by superiors. Hopwood indicated that the rigid budget-constrained style was associated with high degrees of job-related tension and the manipulation of accounting data. The more flexible profit-conscious style was not linked to such detrimental effects. Hopwood concluded that the latter style would lead to greater organisational effectiveness. Otley (1978), in a study of profit centres within the mining industry and using comparable measures to the Hopwood study, suggested that a more rigid style led to better performance. The two studies were set in different industries, so strengthening the contingency theory case, but they also reflected different organisational structures. The Hopwood study was based in an integrative plant with extensive interdependency between cost centres, while the Otley study was concerned with the performance of coal mines which were quite independent of one another.

Baulmer (1971) indicated the inappropriate use of rigid performance measures where extensive interdependency exists between departments. Strict conformance with budgets becomes less appropriate the greater the independence of department or unit. With hindsight this conclusion may appear obvious, but it has important implications for the modern organisation. As the delegation of authority and responsibility is pushed down the organisation, either through strategic processes for the strategic business unit or through the empowerment of employees through TQM adoption, then more flexible performance-measurement systems become the norm. The interrelationships between departments, functions and productive units is so critical to the modern organisation that rigid-style performance measures would lead to the negative attributes associated with the budget-constrained style recognised by Hopwood. The use of cross-function teams for the complementation of many of the modern management techniques, including target costing, ABC, TQM, BPR and so on requires a balanced view of performance that is determinant-focused to achieve appropriate results in performance.

The environment

The theme of flexibility within performance measures and management control systems is continued when the environment is considered as a contingent variable. Burns and Stalker (1961) argue that mechanistic (bureaucratic) information systems are appropriate in stable environments operating with known technologies, while organic (flexible) systems would be appropriate for more uncertain environments with less defined technologies. Chandler (1962) argued that environmental complexity is significantly correlated to the extent of decentralisation, and that a strategy of product diversification has caused many organisations to divisionalise and subsequently form strategic business units.

Ezzamel and Hart (1987) make the following observation: 'Thompson (1967) considered complex organisations as open systems which are indeterminate and faced with uncertainty, but at the same time are rational and seeking a degree of determinateness and certainty. Hence, an organisation's main problem in dealing with its environment is how to rationally handle uncertainty. The organisation can remove, or at least reduce, uncertainty by reducing the number of variables operating on it' (p.29). This can be done by designing specific parts of the organisation to deal with specific uncertainties and others to deal with more certain activities. As well as taking a reflective role, many organisations may seek to influence their environments to reduce the uncertainties present.

Amigoni (1978) summarises the contingency environmental theory issues as follows:

In stable environments,

(a) the more numerous are the business units and the greater is the contact between them, the more detailed the systems must be with an orientation towards output, i.e. products and markets.

(b) The more complex the organisational structure is, the more relevant and selective it will be with regard to the decisional activity of each organisational unit. The degree of detail must be higher at the low levels and lower at the top levels.

(c) The more complex the organisational structure is, the higher the degree of formal responsibility and procedural rigidity and the tighter the style of control will be.

In turbulent environments,

(a) The more discontinuous the environment is, the more the system must be oriented to the future with a high degree of quickness.

(b) The less discontinuous the environment is, the more procedural rigidity should decrease and the style of control change from tight to loose. (p.181)

The modern business operates in dynamic and often unstable environments. There is a need to provide management information that provides a flexible, strategically driven view of the organisation that is sufficiently broad to capture important environmental changes. Equally it is important that performance measurement is future-oriented rather than backward-looking. Both the balanced scorecard of Kaplan and Norton (1992) and the results and determinants framework of Fitzgerald et al. (1991) provide a forward perspective by offering performance measures that may be the constituents required to either maintain or establish comparative competitive advantages.

The general movement of organisations to be more customer-focused in the provision of products and services is a proactive attempt to reduce the instability in the user market, while links with suppliers are an attempt to provide greater stability within the supply chain. Such proactive initiatives mean a change of emphasis for performance measurement that capture the more subjective issues in the building of alliances and managing customer-oriented processes.

Summary

The contingency theory view is that there is no one 'best' way to approach organisational design, accounting information systems and performance-measurement structures, and that any resultant series of frameworks is organisation-specific to reflect its particular combination of contingent variables. This approach does not form a basis for action, but does provide a sufficiently flexible approach to performance measures and other issues that leaves managers with the confidence to design systems that are appropriate for their particular circumstances.

Some chapters within this text have provided insights into techniques which have universal acceptability but which must be modified and moulded to be organisation-specific if they are to provide genuine benefits for that particular organisation. The 'off-the-peg' answer may be wholly inappropriate to an organisational problem.

The establishment of performance-measurement systems that are wrongly focused and too rigid may result in organisational decline. Performance-measurement systems need to be flexible and integrative, considering current activities to maintain short-term stakeholder confidence while containing measures that encourage the development of activities for the long-term viability of the organisation. As the environment becomes more complex and unstable then performance measures must be sufficiently flexible to reflect these discontinuities.

9 The Role of the Management Accountant: A Reappraisal

The new agenda for business organisations is the ability to maintain and enhance comparative competitive advantage in a dynamic and often hostile environment. Key issues within this process are the enhancement of the customer focus, the continual improvement of product and service quality and the reduction of cost. There is a requirement by management to enhance information systems that will capture performance measures that encapsulate on-time delivery, product quality, customer satisfaction, employee morale, profitability, innovative processes, strategic positioning and the like so that an integrated, balanced portfolio of performance measures and reporting mechanisms can be established as a powerful means of managing performance.

Cooper (1996a) argues that, as global competition becomes more intense, firms will seek leaner methods of product and service provision and so will have to become more proactive in the manner in which they manage costs. This has led to new forms of cost management and an adoption of these processes by individuals at all levels within the firm through the notion of 'flatter' management structures and the empowerment of all employees.

With the increased awareness and implementation of cost management processes the management accountant may feel that his or her role within the firm is assured. This would be complacent, however, as many of the cost-reduction-focused techniques are not about product costing but are derived from various non-accounting disciplines including marketing, engineering and computer sciences. The management accountant may not be the natural owner of these new developments or the inheritor of the developing non-financial performance-measurement portfolio.

Kaplan (1995) argues that management accountants should:

- 'become part of their organisation's value-added team;
- participate in the formulation and implementation of strategy;
- translate strategic intent and capabilities into operational and managerial measures; and
- move away from being scorekeepers of the past and become the designers of the organisation's critical management information systems'. (p.13)

Cooper (1996a) argues that there are two ways forward for the management accountant. One is to make the management accounting function more critical to the firm by enhancing the *status quo* and attempting to maintain a monopoly on management information. The second is to take management accounting to the user and actively support the cost management process. This second response involves:

1. 'training as many individuals in the firm as possible in the use of the appropriate management accounting techniques to help those individuals undertake cost management programmes;
2. decentralising much of the management accounting function;
3. developing new management accounting systems to support cost management programmes as they evolve'. (p.31)

The ownership and control of an integrated and appropriate information system within any firm may be a key to the influence of the management accounting role. As the traditional task as the 'keeper of numbers' declines with the introduction of a much broader performance-measurement system aided by improved information systems and simplified production processes, then the role of the management accountant is at the crossroads. Companies require greater insights of their competitive environments and the relative value and costs of competitor offerings as well as internal efficiency measures. All these activities may be done by respective managers within their particular fields of expertise. Management accountants must seek to work with others as cross-team facilitators who can develop systems for performance management that are relevant, integrative and respected by their management users. They must also help to create a company ethos that encourages performance-enhancing and continuous-improvement initiatives than can be integrated into the activities and reflected in the performance-management process.

With particular regard to the integration of a balanced approach to performance measurement, encompassing financial and non-financial information, it may be that the integrity of the non-financial data may be questioned. This is because its preparation may be more subjective than the financial information which is subject to audit trails and accounting control mechanisms. The management accountant, if contributing to a multidisciplinary team, could be the person who ensures the integrity of the non-financial information thus guaranteeing its usefulness within the performance-measurement process while also modifying the management accounting system to reflect operational realities.

In an interesting paper Chenall and Langfield-Smith (1998) considered factors influencing the role of management accounting in the development of performance measures within organisational change programmes. They examined the debate that management accountants should assist and participate in designing performance measures as opposed to non-accountants taking on the role. Management accountants have experience and an established role in evaluating managerial and organisational performance which links process and strategy. However, the involvement of accountants does not always lead to the improved design of performance-measurement systems, as they bring an overly financial focus to the role, so giving a biased view that may be product-oriented rather than process-focused.

The Chenall and Langfield-Smith study focused on a series of case studies in which companies were implementing change programmes that involved the enhancement of customer-satisfaction and cost-reduction programmes to sustain competitive advantage. Specific initiatives involved the development of work-based teams centring on cellular manufacture and company-wide customer-satisfaction programmes. The work-based teams and management realised that the original performance measures required modification to reflect the process orientation and customer focus while including greater budget accountability. The study considered how and if particular management accountants and their departments contributed to the redesign of the performance measures. They suggest the following actions that management accountants must take to be included within the development and management of progressive, balanced performance measures:

1. Management accountants must want to participate actively in performance-management design. They need to be part of a cross-functional team, not just involved with financial data.
2. Broaden the accounting culture so that it complements and fits with other business processes, moving the focus from control to coaching.
3. Gain the confidence of top managers by the demonstration of broader accounting skills through accounting innovations. This should ensure the inclusion of accountants on cross-functional working parties.
4. Provide a service to all managers by contributing to the broader vision of the company through working with operational personnel.
5. Assure managers that accountants are part of any development programme and not merely compliance officers. This may be done through the participation in company-wide training programmes for TQM, JIT and other initiatives, so that accountants become part of the management team rather than separate from it.
6. The formal hierarchy within the business must recognise that accountants need integrating with other managers in terms of office location and product and service delivery.

Management accountants must be considered and recognised as coaches rather than controllers of the performance-measurement agenda if their role is to be sustained and developed within modern business processes.

References

Amigoni, F (1978) 'Planning Management Control Systems', *Journal of Business Finance and Accounting*, 5 (3). Reprinted in Emmanuel, C, Otley, D and Merchant, K (eds), *Readings in Accounting for Management Control*, Chapman & Hall.

Anthony, R N (1965), in Planning and Control Systems: A Framework for Analysis (Boston MA: Graduate School of Business Administration, Harvard University).

Anthony, R N, Dearden, J and Bedford N M (1984), Management Control Systems (5th edn.) (Case study 3–2 General Electricity Company (A) Richard D Irwin Inc.

Argenti, J C (1989), *Practical Corporate Planning*, Unwin

Atkinson, M (1998), British Output is Bound Up by Red Tape, Guardian, 30 October.

Babicky, J. (1996), 'TQM and the Role of CPAs in Industry', *CPA Journal,* March.

Baulmer, J V (1971), 'Defined Criteria of Performance and Organisational Control', *Administrative Science Quarterly*, September.

Bennett, M and James, P (1996),'Environmental-related Performance Measurement in Business', in Baynes, P and Tilley, I (eds), *Contemporary Issues in Performance Measurement*, Greenwich University Press.

Bennett, M and James, P (1998), *Environment Under the Spotlight: Current Practice and Future Trends in Environmental and Related Performance Measurement for Business*, ACCA Research Report No.55.

Binnersley, M (1996), 'Do you Measure Up?' *Management Accounting*, November.

Booth, R (1997), 'Performance Management: Making it Happen', *Management Accounting*, November.

Booth, R (1998), 'Measures for Programmes of Action', *Management Accounting*, July/August.

Brander Brown, J and McDonnell, B (1995), 'The Balanced Scorecard: Short-term Guest or Long-term Resident?', *International Journal of Contemporary Hospitality Management*, 7 (2/3).

Brignall, S, Fitzgerald, L, Johnson, R and Silvestro, R (1991), 'Performance Measurement in Services Businesses', *Management Accounting*, November.

Broadbent, J M and Cullen, J (1995), 'Divisional Control', in Berry, J, Broadbent, J and Otley, D T (eds), 'Management Control: Theories, Issues and Practices' , Macmillan.

Broadbent, J M and Cullen, J (1997), *Managing Financial Resources* (2nd edn), Butterworth-Heinemann.

Bromwich, M and Bhimani, A (1994), *Management Accounting: Pathways to Progress*, CIMA.

Burns, T and Stalker, G M (1961), *Management of Innovation*, Tavistock

Cadbury Report (1992), *Report of the Committee on the Financial Aspects of Corporate Governance*, Gee.

Caulkin, S (1997), 'Stampede to Replace the Principle of Profit', *Observer*, 12 January.

Chandler, A (1962), *Strategy and Structure*, MIT Press.

Chartered Institute of Management Accountants (1991), *Management Accounting: Official Terminology* (2nd edn), CIMA.

Chartered Institute of Management Accountants (1993), *Performance Measurement in the Manufacturing Sector*, Research Studies, CIMA.

Chartered Institute of Management Accountants (1996), *Management Accounting: Official Terminology* (3rd edn), CIMA.

Chenall, R and Langfield-Smith, K (1998), 'Factors Influencing the Role of Management Accounting in the Development of Performance Measures Within Organisational Change Programs', *Management Accounting Research*, 9.

Coates, J B, Davies, E W, Longden, S G, Stacey, R J and Emmanuel, C (1993), *Corporate Performance Evaluation in Multinational Companies*, CIMA.

Coates, J B, Davies, M L, Zafar, A, Davis, E W and Zwirlein, T (1995), Adopting Performance Measures That Count: Changing a Shareholder Value Focus, European Accounting Association Conference paper.

Cooper, R (1996a), 'The Changing Practice of Management Accounting', *Management Accounting*, March.

Cooper, R (1996b), 'Activity-based Costing and the Lean Enterprise', *Journal of Cost Management*, Winter.

Cooper, R and Kaplan, R S (1988), 'Measure Costs Right: Make the Right Decision', *Harvard Business Review*, Sept./Oct.

Corporate Report (1975), Accounting Standards Steering Committee, London.

Crockatt, F (1992), Revitalising Executive Information Systems', *Sloan Management Review*, Summer.

Daft, R L and MacIntosh, N B (1978), 'A New Approach to Design and Use of Management Information', *California Management Review*, Fall.

Dale R G, Lascelles D M, and Plunkett J J (1990) 'The Process of Total Quality Management', in Dale B G and Plunket J J (eds) Managing Quality, April

Dent, J F (1990), 'Process Model of Relationship Between Business Strategy and Management Control Systems: Strategy, Organisation and Control: Some Possibilities for Accounting Research', *Accounting Organisations and Society*, 15 (1/2).

Dinesh, D and Palmer, E (1998), 'Management by Objectives and the Balanced Scorecard: Will Rome Fall Again?', *Management Decision*, 36 (6).

Doyle, P (1994), 'Setting Business Objectives and Measuring Performance', *Journal of General Management*, Winter.

Drew, S A W (1997), 'From Knowledge to Action: The Impact of Benchmarking on Organisational Performance', *Long Range Planning*, 30.

Drucker, P F (1988), 'The Coming of the New Organisation', *Harvard Business Review*, Jan./Feb.

Drucker, P F (1989), *Practice of Management*, Heinemann.

Drury, C (1985), *Management and Cost Accounting*, Van Nostrand Reinhold.

Dunlop, A (1998), *Corporate Governance and Control*, CIMA.

Euske, K J, Lebas, M J and McNair C J (1993), 'Performance Measurement in an International Setting', *Management Accounting Research*, 4.

Emmanuel, C R, Otley, D T and Merchant K (1990), *Accounting for Management Control* (2nd edn), Chapman & Hall.

Evans, H, Ashworth, G, Gooch, J and Davies, R (1996), 'Who Needs Performance Management?', *Management Accounting*, December.

Ezzamel, M, Green, C, Lilley, S and Willmott, H (1995), 'Changing Managers and Managing Change', CIMA.

Ezzamel, M and Hart, H (1987), *Advanced Management Accounting: An Organisational Emphasis*, Cassell

Fitzgerald, L, Brignall, S, Johnston, B and Markon, E (1998), 'Continuous Improvement and Radical Change: A Question of Degree?', *Performance Measurement: Theory and Practice*, Centre for Business Performance University of Cambridge.

Fitzgerald, L, Johnston, R, Brignall, S, Silvestro, R and Voss, C (1991), *Performance Measurement in Service Businesses*, CIMA.

Fitzgerald, L and Moon, P (1996), *Performance Measurement in Service Industries: Making it Work*, CIMA.

Freund, Y P (1988), 'Critical Success Factors', *Planning Review*, 16 (4).

Goold, M and Campbell, A (1987), 'Managing Diversity:Strategy and Control in Diversified British Companies', *Long Range Planning*, 20 (5).

Govindarajan, V and Gupta, A K (1985), 'Linking Control Systems to Business Unit Strategy: Impact on Performance', *Accounting Organisations and Society*, 10 (1).

Grant, R M (1995), *Contemporary Strategic Analysis: Concepts, Techniques, Applications* (2nd edn), Blackwell.

Gray, R, Bebbington, J and Walters, D (1993), *Accounting for the Environment*, ACCA/Paul Chapman.

Greenbury Report (1995), *Report of The Committee on the Review of Directors' Remuneration*, Gee.

Hall, R (1993), 'A Framework Linking Intangible Resources and Capabilities to Sustainable Competitive Advantage', *Strategic Management Journal*, 14.

Hall, W K (1978), 'SBUs: Hot New Topic in the Management of Diversification', *Business Horizons*, February.

Hopwood, A G (1972), 'An Empirical Study of the Role of Accounting Data in Performance Evaluation', *Empirical Research in Accounting*, supplement to *Journal of Accounting Research*.

Horngren, C T, Bhimani, A, Foster, G and Datar, S M (1999), *Management and Cost Accounting*, Prentice Hall Europe.

Innes, J (1995), 'Activity Performance Measures and the Tableaux de Bord', in Lapsley, I and Mitchell, F (eds), *Accounting and Performance Measurement*, Paul Chapman.

Innes, J and Mitchell, F (1990), *Activity Based Costing – Review with Case Studies*, CIMA.

Institute of Internal Auditors (1996), *Business Process Re-engineering*, Professional Briefing Note No.9.

Johnson, G and Scholes, K (1997), *Exploring Corporate Strategy, Text and Cases* (4th edn), Prentice Hall.

Johnson, H T and Kaplan, R S (1987), *Relevance Lost: The Rise and Fall of Management Accounting*, Harvard Business School Press.

Kaplan, R S (1995), 'New Role for Management Accountants', *Journal of Cost Management*, Fall.

Kaplan, R S and Norton, D P (1992), 'The Balanced Scorecard – Measures That Drive Performance', *Harvard Business Review*, 70 (1).

Kaplan, R S and Norton, D P (1996), *The Balanced Scorecard: Translating Strategy Into Action*, Harvard Business School Press.

Laughlin, R and Gray, R (1988), *Financial Accounting – Method and Meaning*, Van Nostrand Reinhold.

Lebas, M (1993), 'Tableaux de Bord and Performance Measurement', Conference Paper, Management Accounting Research Group, London School of Economics, April.

Lowe, E A and Soo, W F (1980), 'Organisational Effectiveness – A Critique and Proposal', *Managerial Finance*, 6 (1).

Mayle, D T, Francis, G A J, Hinton, C M and Holloway J A (1998), 'What Really Goes on in the Name of Benchmarking?' *Performance Measurement Theory and Practice*, Centre for Business Performance, Cambridge.

McKinsey Report (1998), Driving Productivity and Growth in the UK Economy, McKinsey Global Institute.

McNair, C J, Lynch, R L and Cross, K F (1990), 'Do Financial and Non-Financial Performance Measures Have to Agree?', *Management Accounting* (US), November.

Miles, R E and Snow, C C (1978), *Organisational Strategy, Structure and Process*, McGraw-Hill.

Mintzberg, H (1983), *Power in and Around Organisations*, Prentice Hall.

Mouritsen, J (1998), 'Driving Growth: Economic Value Added Versus Intellectual Capital', *Management Accounting Research*, 9.

Murphy, M (1998), 'Using the Balanced Scorecard for More Efficient Commissioning', *British Journal of Medical Care*, 3 (9).

Newing, R (1995), 'Wake up to the Balanced Scorecard', *Management Accounting*, March.

Nichols, P (1998), 'Unlocking Shareholder Value', *Management Accounting*, October.

O'Hanlon, J (1997), *An Earnings-based Valuation Model in the Presence of Sustained Competitive Advantage*, working paper, Lancaster University.

O'Hanlon, J and Peasnell, K (1998), 'Wall Street's Contribution to Management Accounting: the Stern Stewart EVA™ Financial Management System' *Management Accounting Research*, 9.

Otley, D T (1978), 'Budget Use and Managerial Performance', *Journal of Accounting Research*, No 16.

Otley, D T (1997), 'Better Performance Measurement', *Management Accounting*, January.

Pearce, J A and Robinson, R B (1985), *Strategic Management, Strategy Formulation and Implementation*, Irwin.

Piper, J (1978), 'Determinants of Financial Control Systems for Multiple Retailers: Some Case Study Evidence', unpublished paper, University of Loughborough

Porter, M E (1985), *Competitive Advantage*, Free Press.

Rappaport, A (1986), *Creating Shareholder Value: The New Standard for Business Performance*, Free Press.

Reece, J S and Cool, W R (1978), 'Measuring Investment Centre Performance', *Harvard Business Review*, May–June.

Reich, R B (1991), *The Work of Nations*, Alfred A Knopf.

Roberts, M W and Silvester, K J (1996), 'Why ABC Failed and Why it May Yet Succeed', *Journal of Cost Management*, Winter.

Scarlett, R (1997), *Value-based Management*, CIMA.

Scott, B R (1971), 'Four Stages of Corporate Development – Part 1', *Harvard Business School Case Services*

Scott, P (1996), 'Benchmarking', *Management Accounting*, July/August.

Shillinglaw, G D (1982), *Cost Accounting Analysis and Control*, Irwin.

Simmonds, K (1981), 'Strategic Management Accounting', *Management Accounting*, April.

Simons, R (1987), 'Accounting Control Systems and Business Strategy: An Empirical Analysis', *Accounting, Organisations and Society*, 12 (4).

Society of Management Accountants of Canada (1993a), *Benchmarking*, Management Accounting Guideline No.16 .

Society of Management Accountants of Canada (1993b), *Implementing Just-in-Time Production Systems*, Management Accounting Guideline No.19.

Society of Management Accountants of Canada (1994), *Developing Comprehensive Performance Indicators*, Management Accounting Guideline No.31.

Society of Management Accountants of Canada (1997), *Measuring and Managing Shareholder Value Creation*, Management Accounting Guideline No.44.

Soin, K (1995), 'Management Control in the Financial Services Sector', in Berry A J, Broadbent, J and Otley, D T (eds), *Management Control: Theories, Issues and Practices*, MacMillan.

Solomons, D (1965), *Divisional Performances: Measurement and Control*, Irwin.

Tanaka, M, Yoshikawa, T, Innes, J and Mitchell, F (1993), *Contemporary Cost Management*, Chapman & Hall.

Thompson, J D (1967), *Organisations in Action*, McGraw-Hill.

Tomkins, C (1973), *Financial Planning in Divisionalised Companies*, Haymarket.

Vancil, R F (1979), *Decentralisation: Ambiguity by Design*, Wiley.

Whittaker, A (1992), 'The Transformation in Work: Post-Fordism Revisited, in Reed, M and Hughes, M (eds), *Rethinking Organisation: New Directions in Organisational Theory and Analysis*, Sage.

Williamson, O E (1970), *Corporate Control and Business Behaviour*, Prentice Hall.

Williamson, O E (1975), *Markets and Hierarchies: Analysis and Antitrust Implications*, Free Press.

Wilson, R M S (1991), 'Strategic Management Accounting', in Ashton, D, Hopper, T and Scapens, R W (eds), *Issues in Management Accounting*, Prentice Hall.

Wilson, R M S (1994), 'Criteria for Measuring Marketing Performance', paper presented at the Performance Measurement and Control Seminar, CIMA Research Foundation.

Wilson, R M S and Chua, W F (1993), *Managerial Accounting: Method and Meaning* (2nd edn), Chapman & Hall.

Woodward, J (1965), *Industrial Organisation: Theory and Practice*, Oxford University Press.

Wright, G (1998), 'Perspectives on Performance Measurement Conflicts in Service Businesses', *Journal of General Management*, 23 (4).

Index